Praise for *Powerful Student Care:*
Honoring Each Learner as Distinctive and Irreplaceable

Finally, a book that cuts through the noise and helps us return to the human side of teaching. *Powerful Student Care* challenges us to listen differently, understand more fully, and learn more deeply about the entirety of a student's experience as a learner. A wonderfully practical, insightful, and inspiring resource.

—Alisa Simeral, author, school turnaround specialist, and veteran educator

This book forces educators to reflect on widely accepted beliefs and practices that exclude and marginalize students. The roadmap and protocols that are presented allow practitioners to bridge theory and practice, encouraging immediate action. The concept of Powerful Student Care is essential if we, as educators, wish to see our students' full potential realized.

—Sara Monaco, EdD, Assistant Superintendent, Smithfield Public Schools

Powerful Student Care is a unique book, not just in what it covers, but also in how it guides, incorporates, and ultimately absorbs the reader. It is comprehensive with regard to knowledge imparted, and takes readers on a journey to five ports of call to establish strong and deep student care. Within the storyline, the readers become part of the plot: first by considering examples provided by the authors, and then, from the very beginning, being invited frequently to "take the helm" with clear and interesting case studies to address. There are seven essential tools in the Appendix that further support self-learning and application. Chandler and Budge have given us a book to be read, savored, and immediately used—all in the service of Powerful Student Care.

—Michael Fullan, Professor Emeritus and former Dean, Ontario Institute for Studies in Education, University of Toronto

Through their skillful maritime metaphor, Drs. Chandler and Budge sagely bring awareness to the oft-acknowledged but under-addressed problem of allowing our assumptions—the lenses formed through our own voyages in life, the cognitive schemas that shape the ways in which we make meaning—to pull us off course in our journey to build student resilience and self-efficacy. *Powerful Student Care* provides us with a way of being, a way of knowing, and a way of thinking that encourage us to not just do what we've always done, to set aside our personal biases, and to expand our understanding in a way that allows us to remain focused on THE STUDENT, where our focus belongs. PSC is freeing, unbinding in that it forces us to own the access, participation, and growth of every student, regardless of our role. And through our own professional efficacy, we give students the opportunity to build their own. It's not about me. It's about the student before me.

—Eric Dool, Director of Student Services, West Clermont School District

Like all successful conceits, the one that Grant and Kathleen have developed—the Powerful Student Care Maritime Institute—tells a known truth in a new and revelatory way. When each of us chooses to teach others, we invariably take on an array of responsibilities that goes far beyond the immediately visible concerns of the content we seek to impart. When we choose to teach, we meet face-to-face the potential and promise of a voyage that can serve to transform others' sense of themselves. The PSC Maritime Institute has endeavored to explicitly document each of the ports of call on such a voyage, as well as the harbor toward which we must navigate. The authors have with great care and love written clearly and specifically *why* we must prioritize these practices. In so doing, they have given us a sexton that every educational captain will prize . . . an essential navigational tool for co-creating the voyage each of our learners deserves.

—Michael Pipa, retired public educator/education consultant

We applaud Chandler and Budge for challenging all of us to establish an educational world that ensures every student knows they are "distinctive and irreplaceable." This is an essential cornerstone of an educational system in which the voices of students are listened to, learned from, and acted upon together—for the good of the whole. This timely and inspirational read provides practical guidance and valuable strategies for educators seeking to cultivate school systems where each and every student can achieve their aspirations.

—Dr. Russ Quaglia and Dr. Lisa Lande,
Quaglia Institute for School Voice and Aspirations

Grant and Kathleen have strengthened my resolve as an educator. Their call to rip to shreds anything that dehumanizes students ignites my passion for being a part of the distinctive and irreplaceable lives of the children with which we are entrusted in every educational space. I am deeply grateful to be invited to the table to be a part of the conversation that is focused on understanding each student's dignity and worth.

—Katherin L. Mohney, 22-year educator—teacher, principal,
central office administrator, superintendent, consultant

If you need convincing that each of our students needs to feel valued and respected while experiencing joy while learning, well, move along to another profession. For the rest of us, this book is a treasure trove of "how-to" strategies and structures to help do just that. We have a lot of ingrained practices in education—as a system, and as individuals—that don't accomplish the goals they're purported to address. Kathleen and Grant encourage us to confront that reality and take steps to rectify our approaches. This ought to get the wheels turning!

—Pete Hall, author, *Always Strive to Be a Better You:
How Ordinary People Can Live Extraordinary Lives*

Powerful Student Care (PSC) is the solution to educating today's students. PSC suggests that you look at yourself, your words, your actions, and your beliefs before trying to extend the tenets of community to our youth. The strategies and stories discussed within this book are challenging, reflective, and powerful for student growth, philosophical growth, and personal growth. I believe this philosophy and mindset could be the start to an evolution of education as we know it!

—Scott Martin, elementary principal

Powerful and insightful! This work reminded me of the voices and actions that my favorite teachers used during my school journey as an immigrant student. Those teachers helped me become who I am today. In this book, you will find personal stories to move you to connect with and empathize with your students, to understand their social and emotional needs. The strategies presented are actionable to help you have a profound impact on your students' learning as well.

—Maria Gonzalez, ASCD Faculty, MG Educational Consulting

Powerful Student Care is what all educators should be reading right now! Chandler and Budge provide the framework for putting learners, in all their uniqueness, at the forefront of learning. As schools continue to recover from the impact of the pandemic, *Powerful Student Care* reminds us it takes an entire school community to support students' social-emotional growth so each child can experience the joy of learning.

—Melanie Ulinger, Director of Curriculum & Special Education, Brocton Central School District

I believe in community. I believe in *each*. I believe each must experience belonging within community in order to realize they are beautifully and wonderfully made—made with promise and purpose. Do you? *Powerful Student Care* is the answer to embracing *each*. As a nana, mom, spouse, teacher, principal, and superintendent of schools, I implore you to discover Powerful Student Care and the power of *each!*

—Penny J. Brockway, teacher, middle school principal, central office administrator, superintendent, consultant

For the past 20-plus years of my educational career, my *why* has remained constant: Create a community in which each child has a safe, caring, environment in which to thrive. During that time, I have read and tried many strategies to meet my goal. However, Powerful Student Care is the only one to provide the *how* to meet the *why*.

—Dianne Wolford, ELA teacher and principal

What Chandler and Budge bring to the table in *Powerful Student Care* is a solution that targets one of the root causes of societal challenges today: inequity in education. Their work points out that until our educational structures, classroom pedagogy, and school district focus recognize that each student matters, nothing else is important. *Powerful Student Care* lays out a system to make sure every child that walks through the door of a school building knows they are welcome, respected, and that they will receive the best the school has to offer, regardless of their socioeconomic background, their race, or any other variable. The bottom line is that each child will understand that they matter! What's refreshing about this work is that it skips the criticism and blame, and instead moves directly to solutions. Chandler and Budge's work provides hope for the future. If embraced, this work will change our world.

—Paul Soma, retired superintendent

POWERFUL STUDENT CARE

ASCD MEMBER BOOK

Many ASCD members received this book as a member benefit upon its initial release.

Learn more at: **www.ascd.org/memberbooks**

GRANT A. **CHANDLER** · KATHLEEN M. **BUDGE**

POWERFUL STUDENT CARE

**Honoring
Each Learner as
Distinctive and
Irreplaceable**

Arlington, Virginia USA

2800 Shirlington Road, Suite 1001 • Arlington, VA 22206 USA
Phone: 800-933-2723 or 703-578-9600 • Fax: 703-575-5400
Website: www.ascd.org • Email: member@ascd.org
Author guidelines: www.ascd.org/write

Penny Reinart, *Deputy Executive Director;* Genny Ostertag, *Managing Director, Book Acquisitions & Editing;* Stephanie Bize, *Acquisitions Editor;* Mary Beth Nielsen, *Director, Book Editing;* Miriam Calderone, *Editor;* Thomas Lytle, *Creative Director;* Donald Ely, *Art Director;* Melissa Johnston/The Hatcher Group, *Graphic Designer;* Valerie Younkin, *Senior Production Designer;* Kelly Marshall, *Production Manager;* Shajuan Martin, *E-Publishing Specialist;* Christopher Logan, *Senior Production Specialist*

PAPERBACK ISBN: 978-1-4166-3191-0   ASCD product #123009

PDF EBOOK ISBN: 978-1-4166-3192-7; see Books in Print for other formats.

Quantity discounts are available: email programteam@ascd.org or call 800-933-2723, ext. 5773, or 703-575-5773. For desk copies, go to www.ascd.org/deskcopy.

ASCD Member Book No. FY23-6 (Apr. 2023 PSI+). ASCD Member Books mail to Premium (P), Select (S), and Institutional Plus (I+) members on this schedule: Jan, PSI+; Feb, P; Apr, PSI+; May, P; Jul, PSI+; Aug, P; Sep, PSI+; Nov, PSI+; Dec, P. For current details on membership, see www.ascd.org/membership.

Library of Congress Cataloging-in-Publication Data
Names: Chandler, Grant A., author. | Budge, Kathleen M., author. Title: Powerful student care : honoring each learner as distinctive and irreplaceable / Grant A. Chandler and Kathleen M. Budge.
Description: Arlington, VA : ASCD, [2023] | Includes bibliographical references and index.
Identifiers: LCCN 2022059148 (print) | LCCN 2022059149 (ebook) | ISBN 9781416631910 (paperback) | ISBN 9781416631927 (pdf)
Subjects: LCSH: Students—Psychology. | Individuality in children. | Belonging (Social psychology) in children. | Teacher-student relationships. | School environment.
Classification: LCC LB1083 .C38 2023 (print) | LCC LB1083 (ebook) | DDC 371.102/3—dc23/eng/20230126
LC record available at https://lccn.loc.gov/2022059148
LC ebook record available at https://lccn.loc.gov/2022059149

32 31 30 29 28 27 26 25 24 23   1 2 3 4 5 6 7 8 9 10 11 12

POWERFUL STUDENT CARE

Honoring Each Learner as Distinctive and Irreplaceable

Foreword

In my early days of working with educators to introduce the concepts of the Innocent Classroom, I became convinced that the world of education was divided into two groups of leaders: those who believed that curriculum and pedagogy were sufficient to provide a quality education, and those who believed that relationships with students were the basis for success in the classroom. Even in districts and schools where relationships were a part of school culture, academic and behavioral results were often disconnected from the health and quality of the relationships between teachers and students.

It does my heart good to see so many educators now articulating the necessity of building relationships with students and, for me, with Black, Brown, and Indigenous children, in ways that welcome and ignite the academic fire lurking in our children's reality.

Before anything and throughout everything, we should know the children we teach.

Books like *Powerful Student Care* move us further into understanding how to accomplish this rather delicate and difficult task. Grant Chandler and Kathleen Budge offer a wonderful blueprint to get us going. They outline the details of the challenge and new approaches to achieving the goal of reaching the powerful place where we know the children we teach well enough to understand and respond to them appropriately.

We educators are often surprised when we find ourselves struggling to know each of our students well enough to lead them, to influence them, to teach them. Many of us believe the deep compassion and commitment we bring to school should be enough to help us accomplish these goals. But compassion and commitment are natural qualities for educators, and, in our contemporary culture, they are often not enough. Knowing the children in a classroom requires more than our individual histories have taught us.

The most beautiful thing to watch is an educator who has done the work and begins to engage with their students in a way that reflects their understanding of those students. It often requires more than the innate quality of caring. It is a skill, one that invites exploration.

This book provides that exploration through Powerful Student Care: a "humanizing approach to education that allows for introspection and reflection; hones our capacity to observe, question, and analyze information; and guides us to use our professional expertise to deeply know each child and predict, plan for, and respond to collective and individual interests and needs." Indeed, in this book you will be asked to go on an allegorical journey to a place the authors call The Harbor. Along the way, you will discover and experience the elements and ways of thinking that will make your trip successful. When you've arrived at your destination, you'll know you've engaged in the right amount of reflection and preparation to know your students better.

The authors believe—as do I—that we expend too much energy trying to manage our students and not enough trying to understand their realities and constructing environments that allow them to drop the barriers that make it more difficult for them to learn. *Powerful Student Care* walks you through an incisive and well-thought-out progression from the rationale and research behind Powerful Student Care to detailed case studies to exercises that invite you to reflect on and respond to classroom scenarios.

I am particularly moved by the authors' discussion about expectations of student performance. In the work that we do, it is critical that teachers not assume that poor performance stems from a lack of interest or desire. When we know our students well, it is easier to understand poor performance in relation to the challenges a student may be facing both inside and outside the school. In many ways, this insight is the goal of every educator who prioritizes relationship, because once we know some of the reasons a child is underperforming, we are able to change that dynamic in our classrooms. To do so, we have to believe our children want to perform well and would do so under different circumstances. As the authors tell us, "Believing in our students' innate intention to do well isn't just something we *should* do; it is something we *must* do."

Altogether, this book is a sharp, articulate conversation about developing relationships with students, with plenty of tools to plan and engage. Any educator who is committed to their students' continued growth will find in *Powerful Student Care* a treasure befitting the journey.

—Alexs Pate

Acknowledgments

From Grant

A few years ago, I had the absolute pleasure to meet Wyatt, a transgender man in his early 20s. It was fascinating and eye-opening to learn about his story. I was completely impressed by this young man's courage to live his authentic life and to present to the world his truth, his passion, and his desire simply to be acknowledged, accepted, and appreciated for exactly who he is. He was demanding to be seen, to be listened to, and to be valued. I was in awe of his kindness, his sensitivity, and his gentle but firm desire for social justice. At his age, as a gay man, I lacked the courage he demonstrated every day just by living his life in such a genuine, open, and honest fashion.

I wondered what Wyatt's life would have been like if he had not waited for adulthood to begin outwardly presenting his authentic self to the world. I especially wondered how the educational community and his fellow students would have responded to him. How, if at all, would they have supported him? And I thought about all the ways schooling fails to value and nurture each student's developing identity and to safeguard each student's human dignity.

My "wonderings" about Wyatt are at the heart of the way in which Kathleen and I have conceptualized Powerful Student Care. I have long believed our children need us to rethink the way we do school. For some, our success in doing so is a matter of life and death. I wholeheartedly agree with a colleague who said, "No one dies here on my watch."

I would like to thank Kathleen for joining me on this journey. It has been a tremendous honor to share this concept of Powerful Student Care with you and to develop it together into a practical, doable way of being, knowing, and thinking. Thank you for your wisdom, friendship, and the dedication we share for each student to believe they are distinctive and irreplaceable.

From Kathleen

Grant and I agree: the need to rethink schooling is a matter of life and death for many students. Years ago, I read the book *There Are No Children Here: The Story of Two Boys Growing Up in the Other America* by Alex Kotlowitz (1991). I remember how struck I was by the way the children spoke of their hopes, dreams, and aspirations for their future. Rather than saying, for example, "I want to become a scientist *when* I grow up, they said, "I want to become a scientist *if* I grow up." They had learned (in school and beyond) that people who looked like them and shared their experiences may or may not live to grow up.

Although education alone will not cure all the ills of society, my work (together with Bill Parrett) in high-performing, high-poverty, racially diverse schools has solidified my conviction that a quality education and committed, caring educators can, and do, make a vitally important positive difference in the lives of students. Thus, I was excited when Grant asked me to engage with him in further conceptualizing Powerful Student Care.

Grant and I have been friends and colleagues for nearly a decade. My appreciation for his enthusiasm and passion continued to grow as we began to examine existing research and draw upon successful practice to imagine what it could mean if schooling was designed to keep us (students and educators) in touch with the undeniable fact that we are each distinctive and irreplaceable. As we asked ourselves what children would need to experience as individuals, and collectively, to believe in their own preciousness and that of others and we attempted to answer that question, I was grateful for Grant's courage to challenge our thinking. Thank you, Grant, for the opportunity to learn and create together. I am indebted to you, my friend.

From Both of Us

This book came to fruition because we had the support of many people. In no case was this truer than the love, support, and countless sacrifices our spouses, James and Bill, made to make this book a reality. We are tremendously grateful for their patience with late-night text sessions, last-minute Zoom meetings, the stress of deadlines, and immeasurable hours when we simply weren't available because we were in the "flow" of creating something we hoped would make a difference for students and the educators who support them. We are also enormously thankful for the love and support of our children. Grant's children and their partners are Julien and Kendall, Holden and Rae. Kathleen's children are Nathaniel, Lindsey, Katrina, A.J., Mia, Ahijah, Jonathan, and Elsa. Kathleen (aka Mimi) also wants her grandchildren, Lukas, Kennedy, Adley Jo, and Finnegan, to know she is ready to play again!

We are extremely grateful to a group of educators who have thought with us, learned with us, challenged our thinking, and read multiple iterations of this work. Your insightful contributions have strengthened Powerful Student Care. We are greatly appreciative of how you strive to extend the five tenets of Powerful Student Care to your students every day. A heartfelt thank-you in particular goes to Scott Martin, Dianne Wolford, Penny Brockway, and Kathy Mohney for your wisdom, compassion, and friendship, as well as to Paul Soma for your thoughtful support and constant cheerleading, reminding us that Powerful Student Care was the solution we had been seeking in education for such a long time. We are indebted to Michelle Wilson-Banks, one of the best math teachers Grant has ever seen. Although she has not yet read this book, we learned from her steadfast commitment to students, which served as the inspiration for Nichelle. An earnest thank-you also goes to Scott and Dianne for being the inspiration for Stewart and Londyn.

A special word of gratitude goes to a group of scholars whose work informed the development of Powerful Student Care, including Lourdes Alvarez-Ortiz, Diane Lyn Baptiste, Laurie Barron, Warren Berger, David Chavis, Floyd Cobb, Edward Deci, Cynthia Foronda, Paulo Freire, Gail Furman, Paul Gorski, Judie Haynes, Donna Hicks,

Patti Kinney, Paula Kluth, Alfie Kohn, John Krownapple, Kien Lee, David McMillan, Jann Murry-Garcia, Kristen Olson, Kevin Ousman, William Parrett, Alexs Pate, Russell Quaglia, Maren Reinholdt, Dan Rothstein, Claudia Ruitenberg, Richard Ryan, Luz Santana, Doris Santoro, Peter Senge, Carolyn Shields, Chayla Rutledge Slaton, Melanie Tervalon, Alice Udvari-Solner, and Debbie Zacarian.

A sincere thank-you is extended to ASCD and a phenomenal team in publishing who were willing to listen to a new idea, give it credence, and support us every step of the way. Specifically, we are grateful for the expertise and support of Genny Ostertag, Stephanie Bize, Miriam Calderone, the design team, and the marketing team. Thank you, also, to Bryan Bown, for your enthusiasm about this book and our work.

Introduction

The future of humanity is in our hands.

—The 14th Dalai Lama

When I had been teaching for a few years, one of my students, Shawn, passed away. Shawn's precious life was very short. He was only 4 when he joined our class community. He had a bit of an elfin face and a tall, lanky body for a child his age. He was shy—very shy. He seemed to carry the weight of the world on his tiny shoulders at times, but at other times his toothy smile would light up his face and our entire classroom. Though this was a community of mostly 3- and 4-year-olds, there were also a few 5-year-olds, including Shawn's brother. This was the first preschool class in our district: It was the mid-1980s, and new federal legislation required states to begin educating students with disabilities at age 3. All the students in my class were identified as having developmental delays.

Shawn died of an unidentified infection. He was absent from class on the Thursday before his death. When I returned to class on Monday, I was called to the principal's office, where she explained that he had passed away in the local hospital over the weekend. The principal asked me if I had ever been worried about Shawn's safety or well-being.

At first, I didn't understand what she was asking. She explained that she was just wondering if Shawn had been neglected. I replied, "No, I had never seen signs of neglect." As I think about that question now, I wonder if she asked it because Shawn's parents were poor. I had had several interactions with Shawn's parents and was confident they loved both their sons and did all they could to care for them.

I changed as a person and teacher that year. I became more profoundly aware of the preciousness of life—each person's life. There were empty spaces in our community after Shawn died: the physical space—his cubby, his coat hook, his circle on the rug—and the felt space—the sadness that came from the simple absence of his distinctive and irreplaceable presence. I remember reading Leo Buscaglia's (1982) *The Fall of Freddie the Leaf: A Story of Life for All Ages* to help us all talk about Shawn's death—a tall order for adults, not to mention preschoolers.

—Kathleen

I met Dominique in my ninth year of teaching, when I moved from a small district to a larger urban one. I had been charged with building both a French program and a debate/forensics program in my high school. Dominique was a sophomore when I began my new post. She lived in what she called the "projects"—an apartment complex for low-income residents—with her grandmother. Dominique was in my second-year French class. The school had scheduled forensics (competitive public speaking) into my second-semester schedule, and it was my job to populate it.

When I met Dominique that fall, she seemed like a typical sophomore in this new school I was getting to know. Then one day, out of nowhere, she announced that she loved my class because she was "learning to speak French, but learning more about life." As I learned more about this young woman, I discovered that she desperately wanted to be successful in school. She had a tough exterior and a heart of gold.

I tended to eat lunch in my classroom, as this was a great quiet time to get work done. One day while I was in there at lunchtime, Dominique knocked on the door and asked if she could eat in my room, as she was not a fan of eating in the cafeteria. One day became two, which became three, then other students joined, and soon a small group of students was eating lunch every day in my room. So it was that my coveted quiet work time faded into oblivion.

From multiple conversations, I learned that Dominique was from Chicago. Her mother still lived there, but she was currently living with "Granny." She spoke well of her mother; there was no conflict between them. As I think back now, almost 20 years later, I believe she lived with her grandmother because her family felt it would be better for her to go to school outside Chicago, and this way she could also help take care of Granny, who had been living alone.

A few months into the school year, Dominique became a driving force on the forensics team, which she helped to quickly grow from 0 to 45 members and for which she served as the team's first president. Two years later, Dominique was competing nationally and ranked in the top 20 for her event. The young, uncertain lady I'd met as a sophomore had become a confident student, performer, and leader. She just needed a gentle nudge and someone to value and believe in her while helping her build some important skills along the way.

I will forever remember the team's first tournament in the winter of Dominique's sophomore year. There were about 500 students in the auditorium, and other than the students on our team, no one looked like Dominique. She looked around, eyes wide open and on high alert. She walked up to me and said, "Mr. Chandler, do you realize that we are the only Black students here?" I replied, "Of course I do, Dominique. Just go out there and wow them. Make sure they remember you were here."

I often wonder what Dominique's experiences would have been if she hadn't found that safe place in which to belong. And I often think about how much I've learned about being a human being from her and the many other Dominiques I've had the privilege to know. Dominique taught me the importance of extending humanity and dignity within the educational experience. She and others taught me to understand their experiences as Black students in the Midwest as I never had before, because I *couldn't* understand until they shared those experiences with me, knowing that I wanted to engage with and learn from them.

—Grant

Powerful Student Care: The Time Has Come

When we began to write this book, we reflected on the pivotal events in our careers that put us in intimate touch with the existential fact that each student is distinctive and irreplaceable—indeed, that we are *all* distinctive and irreplaceable. For Kathleen, Shawn's death was certainly one of those events. For Grant, Dominique's story demonstrates the potency of schools and teachers to cultivate students' talents and aspirations, nurture their self-worth, and uphold their dignity.

At the time that we started writing *Powerful Student Care,* educators throughout the United States had just survived 18 months of pandemic schooling due to COVID-19. We hoped the 2021–2022 school year would bring us to the other side of the pandemic, but such was not the case. Educating children during a global pandemic is not something educators signed up for or even trained for. In addition to making miraculous changes to our pedagogy on a dime, finding ways to support students who missed hours of invaluable learning time, covering for absent colleagues, and caring for (and fearing for) our health and that of our families, many of us grieved the loss of grandparents, parents, spouses, children, aunts, uncles, cousins, neighbors, colleagues, and students. Moreover, many of us could not help but be blinded by the spotlight the pandemic shone on the inequities in our world.

What shall we do with all that we have experienced in these unprecedented times? Can the flexibility and resiliency we have demonstrated in the chaos of pandemic schooling give us the confidence and courage to see that we don't have to rely on the way we've always done things in schools? Can it give us the wisdom to commit to not do things the way we have always done them? Might our personal and collective losses awaken us to the preciousness and uniqueness of each human life? And out of that awakening, might we tap back into the moral reasons we became educators by co-creating, with our students, new ways of being together that heal us and sustain us? We are convinced that the answer to these questions is yes, and that the time has come to embrace Powerful Student Care.

What Is Powerful Student Care?

We developed Powerful Student Care (PSC) over nearly a decade of observing and interacting with teachers and principals who were working diligently to solve problems within their schools. Part of a broader continuous improvement framework, PSC is focused on demonstrating to each student that they are both distinctive and irreplaceable.

Distinctive and Irreplaceable

When we were developing PSC, we chose the words *distinctive* and *irreplaceable* very carefully. We were thinking, "What would it mean if we were to eliminate the alienation so many students experience in school every day? What would we want students to believe about themselves and their peers?"

To be *distinctive* is to be unique—to be unlike any other. We want students and educators to celebrate the beauty and uniqueness of each individual. We want individuals to see and to value one another's individual identities and to recognize each soul as invaluable and irreplaceable.

Think about the word *irreplaceable* for a moment. When we truly believe someone is *irreplaceable,* we ascribe tremendous value to that person. They are treasured. They are cherished. They are of infinite importance because there is no other just like them. Envision how very different our world would be if we actually treated one another as though we were each *irreplaceable.*

There is great power in this idea. Synonyms for *power* include *capacity, capability, competence, authority, potential,* and *skill.* Just imagine the motivation and the confidence of students and educators who understand themselves and others to be both distinctive and irreplaceable. What decisions might we make differently if we could see and celebrate one another in this way? How might this awareness of the preciousness of each person's life change the way we all experience school?

From *All* to *Each*

Powerful Student Care realigns the conversation from a focus on *all* students to a focus on *each* student. Of course, we want all our kids to succeed, to be well-behaved, to learn, and to become happy and productive adults. But it is difficult to visualize *all* when you're a teacher or principal in a building of several hundred (or more) students. Who are we really talking about? We often lose sight of *all* and think about *most* instead. It is not unusual to hear educators say it's impossible to reach 100 percent of students, so we should be satisfied with reaching the vast majority. What's worse, it's very difficult to picture the faces of *all*. Individual identities get lost in the semantics of *all*.

Now consider the word *each*. What's required of us to consider *each* student? Certainly, *each* implies all, but it does so from the singular rather than the collective plural. *Each* student: What's their name? How do they identify themselves? Who are they as a unique soul? What do they bring to the table? It's difficult to talk about each student without referring to them by name. And when we think about each student by name, we can't help but visualize their face, their smile, their beautiful eyes, their challenges, their successes, the people who love and care about them, and their dreams. Nkenge is in 3rd grade and wants to be an Olympian just like Simone Biles. Mohammed is in 1st grade and wants to race cars. Olivia, a struggling 5th grader, dreams of being a scientist. Her uncle died of COVID-19 and she wants to eliminate future pandemics from the world.

What Does Powerful Student Care Ask of Us?

We want each student to *feel* they are both distinctive and irreplaceable, and we know such a feeling comes about (or fails to materialize) as a direct result of their experiences within our schools and classrooms, with their peers, and with their teachers. In this book, we ask you to choose your course—to think about and decide whether or not to respond to the call of PSC. If you respond to the call, you are asked to *rip to shreds* anything that dehumanizes students or disregards or disrespects their identity, talents, or potential. When you choose to nurture the infinite potential in each child, there is no way around dismantling any practices or structures that result in limitations, inequities, and injustices.

What Does Powerful Student Care Do for Us?

Powerful Student Care addresses some practical problems educators deal with daily. But more than that, it leads to a sense of self-worth and dignity that comes with educating our students in a humanizing way. Some might call PSC utopian, but we are confident that what we envision is possible. Indeed, that's why we wrote this book.

Powerful Student Care calls our attention to the vital importance of our work as educators and to appreciating that the success of our efforts (or lack thereof) profoundly impacts the actual life of each student we serve. It calls us to act every day with the knowledge that what we do is greater than test scores or reading levels. It calls us to recognize that our work is a matter of life and death for many students. Powerful Student Care calls us to contemplate the roles our professional expertise, intellect, and humanity play in upholding the humanity, dignity, and worth of each child in our care. Put simply, PSC is a way of being, a way of knowing, and a way of thinking.

Our Humanity: A Way of Being

By challenging practices and structures that demoralize and dehumanize students and educators, PSC allows us to bring the boundless beauty of humanity to the enterprise of schooling. Although it asks us to focus on *each* student, it is not an individualistic approach. In fact, such care is only possible in community with others. Therefore, at its core, PSC is about co-creating a sense of community with and among students—and this book is designed to support you in doing so.

Community is about people, a feeling, a set of relationships, and the meeting of common needs (McMillan & Chavis, 1986). Simply filling a school or a classroom with students and educators does not make it a community; rather, schools and classrooms are the contexts in which a sense of community can flourish. In schools and classrooms where students experience a sense of community, mutual respect is fostered, individuals' needs and interests are met, and infinite human potential is unleashed.

The Five Tenets of Community

The following five tenets of community are foundational to Powerful Student Care:

1. Each student is welcomed to be a part of our community.
2. Each student is a valued member of our community.
3. Each student is here to do well.
4. Each student is here to develop self-efficacy and agency.
5. Each student is here to experience the joy of academic, social, and emotional learning.

When these tenets are lived in schools and classrooms, students feel welcomed and valued. They also come to understand that learning is not only about gaining academic skills, but also about joy. Buoyed by the knowledge that we, their teachers, presuppose that they come to school with the intention to do well, they develop self-efficacy and agency. Caring for students in these powerful ways helps them to see themselves as the distinctive and irreplaceable individuals they are and to appreciate that the same is true of their peers. (For a more detailed look at the five tenets of community central to Powerful Student Care, see Appendix A, p. 157.)

Our Expertise: A Way of Knowing

In conceptualizing Powerful Student Care, we have drawn ideas and strategies from a wide range of knowledge related to educational philosophy, cultural humility, belongingness, community building, trauma-sensitive practices, social-emotional learning, equity literacy, antiracism, cultural responsiveness, student voice, restorative justice, poverty and classism, Freirean thought, moral education, self-care, and antibias education. While embracing PSC will not make us experts in any of these fields of knowledge, it is intended to move us beyond traditionally siloed and sometimes deficit-oriented approaches to caring for students to one that embraces the infinite potential of each young life. The PSC approach does this by asking us to think about our professional expertise not as a set of discrete tools in a toolbox but, rather, as a woven cloth of theories and practices that help us support both each individual student and the community of students as a whole. (We elaborate on this way of knowing in Chapter 3.)

Our Intellect: A Way of Thinking

To provide our students with Powerful Student Care, we must commit to introspection and reflection on our beliefs, values, and life experiences. Deeply knowing who we are and who we bring into the classroom is critical. We do this by interrogating our mental models and the implicit biases that they inevitably contain. Too often, our unexamined biases serve as a barrier to educating students as the distinctive and irreplaceable people they are—particularly students of color, students who live in poverty, students who identify as LGBTQIA+, and students with disabilities. Drawing on the work of the Equal Justice Society, veteran teacher Shane Safir (2016) reminds us:

> Biased messages can be framed to speak to the unconscious. As they stack up, the brain uses rapid cognition to assess the humanity, threat, and worth of other human beings. More concretely, the prefrontal cortex lights up when we see someone as "highly human," but it fails to activate when we dehumanize people. (para. 4)

Powerful Student Care is a humanizing approach to education that allows for introspection and reflection; hones our capacity to observe, question, and analyze information; and guides us to use our professional expertise to deeply know each child and predict, plan for, and respond to collective and individual interests and needs. (These characteristics of PSC are discussed in greater detail in Chapter 4.)

PSC draws inspiration from the philosophy of Ubuntu. *Ubuntu* is a Zulu word that means "humanity" and has been translated as "I am because you are" or "I am because we are." This single word acknowledges our common humanity—the universal bond we all share as humans. Here is how Desmond Tutu (1999) explains Ubuntu:

A person with Ubuntu is open and available to others, affirming of others, does not feel threatened that others are able and good, based from a proper self-assurance that comes from knowing that he or she belongs in a greater whole and is diminished when others are humiliated or diminished, when others are tortured or oppressed. (p. 31)

Ubuntu has been used as an informing philosophy in global diplomacy, social welfare, academic research, leadership and politics, social and criminal justice, education, and popular culture. As such, we see Ubuntu as a North Star for PSC, inspiring humanity in classrooms and schools.

Who Should Read This Book?

Although we wrote this book for educators working in any capacity in the school system, our focus is on implementation in classrooms and schools. We are confident that educators who are searching for a robust, compassionate way of thinking about their students and their own well-being, combined with a fierce means of shattering historical barriers to such well-being, will benefit from this book.

Welcome to the Powerful Student Care Maritime Institute

Throughout this book, we elucidate the principles of Powerful Student Care using a maritime metaphor, including a learning voyage on the PSC *Encounter*. Our metaphor begins with the word *harbor,* conceptualizing it as both an action and a place. In the provision of Powerful Student Care, we harbor our students, providing shelter and protection. We also journey to "The Harbor"—a place of security and comfort. This is our final destination, where each student believes they are distinctive and irreplaceable.

This book is divided into two levels. Level 1 (Chapters 1–4) focuses on the conceptual knowledge you need to provide Powerful Student Care to your students. Here you will participate in the PSC Maritime Institute to learn about the features of the model PSC *Encounter*, with its state-of-the art sails, navigational instruments, and safety devices, so that you will be familiar with how to use these features to sail your own PSC vessel.

In Level 2 (Chapters 5–8) of the book, you set sail on the PSC *Encounter*. On board, you have an opportunity to conduct an in-depth exploration of each of the five ports of call—the tenets of community in Powerful Student Care (see Figure I.1)—en route to The Harbor. This learning voyage allows you to see the connection between the theory behind the tenets and examples of the tenets in practice. These intermediate stops provide a chance to observe PSC captains in action as they work to extend the tenets of PSC to their students. Shadowing other PSC captains who have learned or are in the process of learning to successfully steer their own PSC ships serves two purposes: (1) to provide an opportunity to deepen your understanding of each of the tenets and (2) to support you in beginning to form the habits of mind necessary to provide each student with Powerful Student Care. You will not witness the entire journey each captain has undertaken. However, you will observe Stewart and Meredith as they navigate stops at the first two ports of call and Nichelle and Jack as they navigate stops

FIGURE I.1

The Map to The Harbor

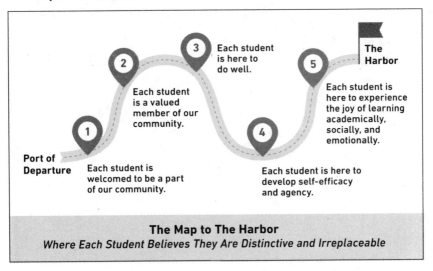

3 Each student is here to do well.

The Harbor

2 Each student is a valued member of our community.

5 Each student is here to experience the joy of learning academically, socially, and emotionally.

1 Port of Departure Each student is welcomed to be a part of our community.

4 Each student is here to develop self-efficacy and agency.

The Map to The Harbor
Where Each Student Believes They Are Distinctive and Irreplaceable

at the final three ports of call. Finally, you will watch Captain Londyn pull it all together as she navigates through each port of call on her way to The Harbor.

We intend the PSC Maritime Institute to prepare you to use your new expertise and knowledge to skillfully navigate constantly changing waters, anticipating any trouble that might throw you off course. In these stormy seas, you will know how to uncover your mental models and explore the roles your intellect, expertise, and humanity play in your professional practice as you gain the navigational aptitude you need to capably steer your PSC ship.

We hope that what you learn from us at the Institute will affirm your thinking and help you to envision yourself and your students together on this voyage. We anticipate that some of what you discover here may cause you to stop and question current or past practices, which could lead you to experience cognitive dissonance, unease, tension, or discomfort. Even so, we will challenge you to accept the call to courageously take each of your students to The Harbor, where they come to believe they are distinctive and irreplaceable. All else, we argue, is secondary.

And so, your journey begins.

~~~~~~~~

The Knowledge Required to Expertly Steer a PSC Vessel

1

Powerful Student Care: Because Each Learner Is Distinctive and Irreplaceable

Every one of us is, in the cosmic perspective, precious.

—Dr. Carl Sagan

We briefly oriented you to the PSC Maritime Institute in the introduction to the book, previewing the preparation we will undertake together to help you become a master captain aboard the PSC *Encounter*. Many of you are experienced captains already. You have navigated your own vessel in both calm and stormy waters, and you are dedicated to bringing your passengers safely and expeditiously to your intended destination.

At the Institute, it is not our intention to teach you how to steer your current vessel and navigate known journeys. You have already proven your ability to do so. Rather, the PSC Maritime Institute offers you a chance to investigate a new vessel and to acquire the navigational skills needed to take the helm of your own PSC ship using the PSC ways of being, knowing, and thinking. You are headed toward The

Harbor, where each student believes that they are distinctive and irreplaceable. Understanding the purpose of PSC training will empower you as captain to work efficiently, to problem-solve as needed, and to anticipate situations we might encounter along the way.

Powerful Student Care: Why This Particular Destination?

Powerful Student Care provides a practical way to bring our expertise, intellect, and humanity into our professional practice. More specifically, PSC addresses three contemporary problems of practice we have found to be universal in our work in schools: the need to

1. Change our conversation about classroom management and discipline,
2. Bring coherence to the many ways we are asked to care for students, and
3. Focus on fixing the system rather than "fixing" the kids.

Powerful Student Care Changes a Conversation That Needs to Change

Perhaps no arena of action requires new ways of doing things more than classroom management. For 25 years, Alfie Kohn has called for our profession to move beyond discipline and management of students, urging us to question the underlying assumptions of most approaches. In a recent blog post, Kohn writes:

> When we are willing to ask the root questions, a qualitatively different kind of classroom comes into focus. It's based on two things: constructing caring classroom and school communities, and giving students more say, individually and collectively, about what they are doing. (2021, para. 8)

Powerful Student Care moves us beyond managing children to creating communities by encouraging us to rethink student expectations, the purpose of discipline, our mental models, and to focus on *each* student rather than *all* students.

Powerful Student Care holds that children come to school needing to learn and hone appropriate social, emotional, and behavior skills, and that it's our job to teach such skills. Too often, educators spend time trying to manage student behaviors rather than teaching and supporting each student to meet appropriate expectations. Whereas managing behaviors means focusing on rules and consequences, supporting each student means striving to ensure that each student has both the skills and the desire necessary to meet expectations (Greene, 2014, 2016).

Powerful Student Care calls us to focus on helping young people regulate their behaviors and develop a sense of agency, moving us away from "managing" students through positive rewards and negative consequences. Powerful Student Care reorients us from thinking about what adults do *to* kids to thinking about what adults do *with* kids. The aim is to help each student gain the self-confidence and skills necessary to make their own choices.

Consider the following scenario (based on a real-life experience of Grant's):

It's near the end of the year, and there's an all-school assembly to celebrate with games and prize giveaways to students who "chose" to meet adults' behavioral expectations. Those in attendance think it's a very exciting, high-energy assembly celebrating children's decisions. There is music playing and balloons decorating the stage as well as all sorts of yummy cookies and cakes beautifully laid out on tables for after the assembly. It's the coolest party they've seen in our school in a long time. Kids are being called to the stage and given prizes from a huge treasure chest that they will take home and enjoy for months to come. Proud family members are taking photos and texting them to other family members and friends who aren't in attendance. There seems to be no limit to the joy and good feelings, and it feels like a really cool time to be a teacher or a leader in this school. Students and parents are beaming. The community has shown tremendous support for the school by providing the amazing prizes.

Now, let's take a second look at this "exciting" event. Look again around the large room. Maybe it's a gymnasium or cafeteria. Does every child have one of these exciting prizes? Is each child holding a game or a toy or clutching the handlebars of a new bicycle? Of course not. This assembly was created by the adults in the school to recognize and reward only those students *who had the skills and knowledge to comply* with school rules and adults' expectations.

Powerful Student Care compels us to examine our underlying assumptions—in essence, to ask ourselves questions such as these:

- Are we solving the right problem?
- Who created these expectations?
- Can each student really *choose* to meet those expectations, or is it that only some have the skills to do so?
- Are the expectations culturally responsive?
- Are students who are not rewarded for meeting expectations disproportionately representative of traditionally marginalized groups?
- Does the current approach result in greater self-regulation or agency for students who need it?
- How do students who don't meet expectations feel when their classmates are rewarded but they aren't?
- Is it productive or counterproductive for some students to leave for the summer feeling less worthy than some of their peers?

In providing each student with Powerful Student Care, we challenge practices that create winners and losers. The adults at the school that held the prize giveaway believed their approach would result in some students "making the right choices" and others failing to do so. They were banking on it—after all, they did not have enough prizes for each student at the event. Even if they had good intentions, they fostered an environment in which some students were an integral part of the school and others were not. Rather than creating events that diminish or even destroy a student's sense of self-worth and dignity, PSC safeguards the inherent dignity of each student to demonstrate that they are distinctive and irreplaceable. No student should have to *earn* this distinction.

At that prize giveaway supposedly for *all* students, where were *each* of these young souls? Did they come to the stage, or did they remain in their seats? When we think about an assembly for *all* kids, we think about them collectively, as a large group. Shifting our thinking to *each* student requires us to see the individual students. Why were Olivia, Nkenge, and Mohammed invited to this event? To be honored, or to watch others be honored? We have a perverse sense that if we recognize the students who are compliant and force those who aren't to watch, this will somehow lead to compliance. Changing the conversation from *all students* to *each student* compels us to notice failed practices, to challenge our thinking about such practices, and to change them.

Coherence in the Many Ways We Care for Students

Much is expected of educators; they must not only continuously develop their content knowledge and their instructional repertoire, but also become trauma-sensitive, culturally responsive, equity-literate, poverty-disrupting, and antiracist. They are also asked to develop the habits of introspection, reflection, critical consciousness, mindfulness, and self-care. Too often, educators view developing each of these competencies as distinct exercises, which can lead them to become overwhelmed.

Powerful Student Care creates coherence among the many ways we are asked to care for students by helping us to view the various strands of our expertise through the prism of five simple tenets for fostering community with and among students. Such a community forms the foundation for PSC focused on providing each student with what they uniquely need, at any given time, to move them forward. These tenets are as follows:

1. Each student is welcomed to be a part of our community.
2. Each student is a valued member of our community.
3. Each student is here to do well.
4. Each student is here to develop self-efficacy and agency.
5. Each student is here to experience the joy of academic, social, and emotional learning.

Powerful Student Care Focuses on Fixing Systems, Not Kids

The COVID-19 global pandemic underscored the inequities that exist in society and in public education. Likewise, the widespread public outcry against racial injustice in the summer of 2021 reminded us all that the roots of these injustices are deep and there is much work to be done before healing can happen. Too many children come to school traumatized by a host of adverse childhood experiences (ACEs), which, for many, come in the form of stereotyping and marginalization based on their race, class, sex, gender, culture, ethnicity, language, immigration status, (dis)ability, or sexual orientation (McKown & Strambler, 2009).

In conceptualizing Powerful Student Care, we acknowledge the inextricable link between the framework and the need to confront and dismantle structural inequities. Living the five tenets requires an ideological commitment that is impossible without a commitment to equity. Powerful Student Care is *a way of being* that begins with the premise that our current educational landscape is inequitable and provides a counternarrative of how classrooms and schools might work. It focuses on transforming structures, processes, and practices rather than on "fixing" kids.

Powerful Student Care Is Good for Teachers Too!

It is undeniable that each educator, like each student, is also distinctive and irreplaceable—but it's not always easy to appreciate that fact in our institutionalized model of schooling. Though educators were hailed as heroes on the frontlines of the COVID-19 pandemic, the teaching profession has a long history of marginalization (Goldstein, 2014). Struggling to meet the demands of state and federal regulations in an unequal system that was never designed to educate all students, some educators have learned to do just enough to get by, while others expect far too much of themselves.

Even before the pandemic, educators were leaving the profession at record rates (Hackman & Morath, 2018), and the situation has only worsened since. Educators of color, in particular, are leaving the profession at higher rates than their white counterparts for two reasons: (1) because they are more affected than their white peers by the degree to which schooling constricts their ability to improve outcomes for low-income students of color and to give back to communities with which they identify, and (2) because too many schools lack "multicultural capital," having "low expectations and negative attitudes about students of color, lack of support for culturally relevant or socially just teaching, and limited dialogue about race and equity" (Achinstein et al., 2010, p. 89).

Doris Santoro (2011) argues that the problem of teacher attrition can be addressed by recognizing what she calls the "demoralization" of educators. Teaching is both an intellectual and a moral endeavor, and Santoro's research demonstrates that educators leave the profession because they feel they can no longer tap into the moral purposes for which they became educators in the first place. These educators view good teaching as more than just helping students achieve academically; to them, good teaching is also about "doing good."

There is no better time than now for educators to embrace Powerful Student Care. It reminds us why we do what we do and why a sense of purpose matters. It also allows us to access the moral rewards of educating young people as it calls us to act from our humanistic commitments. It is made of the stuff that sustains us.

With our destination, The Harbor, clearly on our radar, we now turn our attention to navigating this journey and how best to plot our voyage. We begin with the vessel itself—the space in which we create our way of being.

2
A Way of Being

My humanity is bound up in yours, for we can only be human together.

—Desmond Tutu

As you learn about your role as a PSC captain steering your craft toward The Harbor, it is vital to recognize how different this new ship is from the numerous ships you may have steered previously. We consider the PSC *Encounter* to be a model for all PSC ships, which should be fitted with the same navigational instruments, sails, and safety devices. In this chapter, we present two ideas that are foundational to all Powerful Student Care vessels: *community of difference* and *sense of community*.

On Our Use of the Term *Community*

If we were to ask a group of educators what the terms *classroom community* and *school community* mean, we suspect we would get nearly as many different answers as there are educators in the group. The commonplace use of these terms belies the fact that, as educators, we do not share a common understanding of the concept of *community*. Gail Furman (2002), a scholar who has studied and written extensively on schools as communities, calls our commonplace use of the term "promiscuous" (p. 63) because we have not critically analyzed its meanings and implications for today's schools.

The term *community* as used and understood in education has multiple meanings. Some educators conceptualize community by describing actions they take, such as facilitating team-building activities, using cooperative learning, or conducting "Morning Meetings." Others might speak of the ethos or climate of their school or classroom; still others might describe aspects of school culture, such as the value of caring relationships and the corresponding norms observed in the school.

The term *community* is used to denote groups of students or educators engaged in the act of learning, as in "community of learners" or "professional learning communities." It has also been used to describe various purposes for schooling, such as preparing students for civic participation in "democratic communities."

Notions of community are also linked to schooling models that are in some way connected to the geographic or local culture in which the school is nested (e.g., place-based education, community-based education, outdoor education, Indigenous education). These pedagogies focus on schools *in* community as opposed to school *as* community.

By contrast, Powerful Student Care is primarily concerned with schools and classrooms *as* communities—specifically, communities of difference—as well as with the development of a *sense of community* in students. Here we explore the evolution of the idea of schools as community, including the ways in which a *community of difference* and a *sense of community* have been conceptualized.

What Is Community?

The notion that schools and classrooms should operate like communities rather than organizations is not new. Against the backdrop of the dominant model of schooling in the early 1900s—bureaucratic, depersonalized, and disconnected from local values and culture (which we would argue is still the dominant model)—Dewey (1899/1990) called for developing a sense of community in schools. At the time, his calls "were largely ignored" (Furman, 2002, p. 6); however, the concept reemerged in earnest in the 1980s and 1990s.

Social scientists David McMillan and David Chavis (1986) propose a definition and working theory for a concept they called "a sense of community." They outline four elements in their definition:

1. Membership—a feeling of belonging,
2. Influence—a sense of mattering or making a difference to a group,
3. Integration—a feeling that one's needs will be met through membership in the community, and
4. Shared emotional connection.

Describing how these elements work together, they stress that community is not a place, but rather *a feeling and a set of relationships.*

As schools began to put this theory into practice, a body of knowledge started to emerge pointing to its benefits to students, teachers, and parents. Specifically, the research revealed that a sense of community resulted in higher student achievement, greater student motivation, and improved attendance. Studies related to the development of professional communities among educators have also demonstrated an increased sense of efficacy and greater accountability for student learning on the part of educators (Furman, 2002).

Given such strong evidence, the rightness of the idea that schools and classrooms should function as communities largely went unquestioned (Furman, 2002), though some scholars did begin to question its relevance for contemporary schooling—especially, notions of sameness that are central to much of the theory (Fine et al., 1997; Furman, 2002; Shields, 2002; Shields & Seltzer, 1997). When community is defined by certain shared values, beliefs, and norms, not all students or families are likely to be included. In this way, scholars argue, schools as communities become a "tool of social control" (Furman, 2002, p. 59).

Carolyn Shields (2004), a scholar who had been studying and writing about schools and community for years, introduces the idea of a *community of difference.* Such a conceptualization, she argues, would be more responsive to the realities of contemporary schools.

A Community of Difference

Shields (2004) defines a community of difference as follows:

> Although we generally think of *community* in terms of what binds participants together—shared norms, beliefs, and values—communities of difference are based not on homogeneity but on respect for difference and on the absolute regard for the intrinsic worth of every individual. Members of such communities do not begin with a dominant set of established norms but develop these norms together, with openness and respect, as they share their diverse perspectives. (para. 5)

Shields further notes that the "deliberate and moral" creation of a community of difference is shaped by the following beliefs and values:

- Relationships with all members and among members are the cornerstone.
- Social justice and academic excellence are inextricably intertwined.
- Community members must develop shared understandings of the bedrock moral principles they will use to guide decision making.

Shields (2004) further offers four moral principles that could be used to guide a school's decision making—namely, that education must be just, caring, democratic, and optimistic: "Education that is *just* and *caring* [emphasis added] attends to both the context and outcomes of the learning experience. It considers students' opportunity to learn as well as their achievement.... Education that is democratic and optimistic opens doors of opportunity to all students" (para. 10).

The starting point for fostering a community of difference is the development of deep knowledge of self and others. Shields (2002) explains that, through reflection, educators gain an understanding of "one's own experiences and an explicit understanding of the beliefs, values, and assumptions from which one constructs an understanding of oneself as a teacher and of students as learners" (p. 146). Dialogue engenders an understanding of others and is the "lifeblood" of the community:

> Dialogue is not just talk. It is a way of life—a way of encountering others and treating them with absolute regard. Dialogue is the basis for understanding difference, for celebrating diversity of our school communities, and for creating community with difference rather than ignoring difference. (Shields, 2004, para. 21)

Experiencing belonging in a community of difference is what we mean when we describe Powerful Student Care as a *way of being.* Supporting students in knowing they are distinctive and irreplaceable is the central moral purpose that guides our decision making and compels us to know ourselves and our students deeply. We live in dialogue with our students through our *ways of knowing* (our expertise) and our *ways of thinking* (our intellect). In this context, our students develop a sense of community.

When Students Experience a Sense of Community

In developing a sense of community, we are concerned with ensuring that students have a paramount need met—specifically, their need for relatedness or belonging. "The need for relatedness involves the need to feel securely connected with others in the environment and to experience oneself as worthy of love and respect," writes Osterman (2002). "In essence, then, this need for relatedness is the need to experience belongingness or a sense of community, in a particular context" (p. 168).

Numerous studies have demonstrated that students who experience a sense of community (understood as relatedness and belonging) are more competent and autonomous; are more willing to accept social norms, values, and rules; are more willing to accept responsibility for their behavior; have a higher expectation of success and higher levels of intrinsic motivation; and have a strong sense of identity, self-esteem, and self-efficacy (Allen et al., 2018; Barron & Kinney, 2021; O'Neel & Fuligni, 2013; Osterman, 2002). In turn, this sense of community improves engagement and achievement. The follow-ing shows Osterman's (2002) summary of what matters in a school community:

- When students experience...
    - support from teachers, they view themselves as valued mem-bers of a community.
    - respectful and caring interactions with teachers and peers, they feel worthy of respect and cared for.
    - feelings of being unwelcomed, they are less likely to initiate prosocial behaviors and more likely to withdraw or display aggression.
- Teacher support is most strongly correlated with a sense of community, but peer support is also important.
- Peer acceptance mirrors teacher acceptance. If the teacher is not accepting, peers are less likely to be accepting.
- Relationships between peers are more problematic in terms of a student's sense of community than are relationships between students and teachers.

Tragically, despite our commonplace use of the concept of *com-munity,* its popularity, and the many benefits of students developing a sense of community, many scholars describe schools as "alienat-ing institutions" (Osterman, 2002, p. 169). In fact, Osterman (2002) notes, "There is little evidence that students generally experience their classrooms or schools as welcoming and supportive communi-ties" (p. 172).

A Sense of Community: Popularity and Paradox

With so much evidence that fostering a sense of community meets a fundamental need and results in a plethora of positive outcomes, why do so many students experience school as alienating? One reason may be public schooling's general imperviousness to reform (Tyack & Cuban, 1995). Scholars argue the problem is baked into the system by design. For example, Cobb-Roberts and colleagues (2006) examined the history of public schooling and found that it was designed to be exclusionary. Why? Schools are *de facto* segregated by class, geographical location, and other demographics. The authors provide real-life examples of what they call "imagined community"—places in which the tension between the espoused ideals of citizenship and equality and the realities of exclusion are played out. As Linda Darling-Hammond (1997) points out, schools have never bridged the gap between their ideals and their reality. To do so, they would have to do two things: "teach all students, not just a few, to understand ideas deeply and perform proficiently, and... teach in ways that help different kinds of learners find productive paths to knowledge as they also learn to live constructively together" (para. 13).

Other scholars note that students receive differing levels of support within school and classroom communities. As Osterman (2002) notes, "Research consistently establishes that students receive differential treatment from teachers on the basis of characteristics such as race, gender, class, ability, and appearance, and the differentiation begins early in the school career and increases as students progress through school" (p. 178). Furthermore, teachers' perceptions of student engagement, ability, and academic performance influence the quality of their relationships with students.

We know that both the school environment and the quality and quantity of teacher support play important roles in students' social and emotional well-being as well as in their enjoyment of and engagement in school (Osterman, 2002). In fact, the school context accounts for "as much or more of the variance in students' experience of emotional distress and violence than the family context" (Osterman, 2002, p. 174).

The PSC way of being regards schools and classrooms as communities of difference. Coupling the human need for belonging with the importance of the school context and the role of the teacher, Powerful Student Care helps educators reimagine how to foster a sense of community in each student through the five tenets of community discussed later in this chapter.

Aboard the PSC *Encounter*: Creating a Sense of Community

Gail Furman (2002) reminds us that "all discussion of school community boils down to this fact: 'community' is an affective experience or psychological state" (p. 11). In 1986, McMillan and Chavis described a sense of community as "a feeling that members have of belonging, a feeling that members matter to one another and to the group, and a shared faith that members' needs will be met through their commitment to be together" (p. 9). Decades later, Chavis and Lee (2015) distilled these ideas down to their essence by defining community as "both a feeling and a set of relationships" among people (p. 1).

On ships like the PSC *Encounter*, captains employ state-of-the-art navigation tools to steer the craft, safeguarding a stayed course regardless of weather conditions. Safely navigating the ship to each of the five ports of call on the way to The Harbor, the captains facilitate the creation of a sense of community in multiple ways using the following navigational instruments (see Figure 2.1, p. 30):

1. Structures (e.g., physical environment, use of time, provision of resources), processes, routines, and rituals;
2. Methods of instruction (e.g., cooperative learning, Socratic seminars, collaborative academic discourse), including feedback and support (e.g., personalized feedback, being "on the same team" as the student);
3. Curriculum;
4. Power-sharing relationships (e.g., students having voice in their learning and the ability to make choices; self-efficacy and agency as the goal for students); and
5. Values (e.g., it's safe to fail because we learn from failure; persistence is needed to learn; we are all in this together).

Students' experiences and how they feel about themselves and others serve as our navigational beacons. This distinguishes Powerful Student Care from other approaches to community building that emphasize the attributes of community or the actions taken by adults (Furman, 2002).

FIGURE 2.1

Navigational Instruments for Creating Community

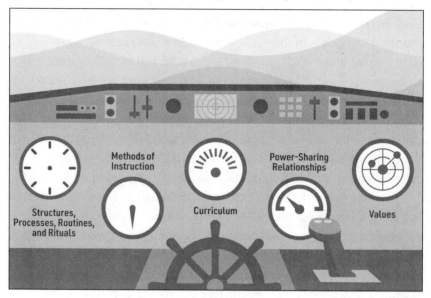

Our Route to The Harbor: The Five Tenets of Community

A skilled captain doesn't leave port without plotting a course, and our students will not believe they are distinctive and irreplaceable unless we use a powerful map to get them there. The five tenets of community central to Powerful Student Care plot the course to The Harbor.

The five tenets illuminate our moral purpose to prove to each student that they are both distinctive and irreplaceable. In Figure 2.2, the tenets are expressed both in language from us to the student—what we want each child to experience every day in every classroom—and in language to us from the student—what we want to hear from and observe in each child once they've internalized a tenet.

In the next chapter, we examine the sails of the PSC *Encounter*, which provide a framework for thinking about the bodies of knowledge that can move this ship through choppy water and offer a way of knowing to navigate what are often turbulent seas.

FIGURE 2.2

The Five Tenets of Community

Each Student Is Supported Uniquely as Each Is Distinctive and Irreplaceable		
"There is no one else like you in our community."		
The Tenet	**What We Say Directly to Students**	**What We Want Students to Say Directly to Us**
Each student is welcomed to be part of our community.	"We want you to feel you belong here."	"I am home. I belong. I have friends. I feel connected to the people here. I know people care for me and I care for them."
Each student is a valued member of our community.	"We can't be as good as we are together without you."	"You care about what I have to say. I have a seat at the table, and I am heard. I can be who I am. I can become who I am."
Each student is here to do well.	"We know you come here every day wanting to do well."	"I am here because I want to do well, and I know you will help me do well. I am trusted. I am capable. I am supported."
Each student is here to develop self-efficacy and agency.	"We want each of you to believe in your own ability to thrive as much as we do."	"I can do this. I am confident. I have power."
Each student is here to experience the joy of learning academically, socially, and emotionally.	"We want you to think that what you are learning is interesting, that it challenges you in just the right way, and that it is relevant to your life."	"This is the place where I learn and grow. This is the place that stretches me. I am motivated here. I am excited here. I am curious here. I feel wonder. I find purpose here."

3

A Way of Knowing

I did then what I knew how to do. Now that I know better, I do better.

—Dr. Maya Angelou

Thus far, we have detailed the reasons for sailing to The Harbor, toured the state-of-the-art vessel you will use for the journey, and inspected the navigational instruments on board. Now, we turn to the sails of the PSC *Encounter*. These sails augment the navigational instruments, enabling our navigation to be more targeted and efficient.

Pay close attention to the weave of the fabric of the sails. Notice the careful design, with horizontal and vertical strands going over and under one another in an alternating pattern. This solid weave design reinforces the strength of each strand and creates the stable, resilient surfaces that form the sails of our ship. On the PSC *Encounter*, these threads weave together theory, research, and successful practice.

The Fabric of Our Sails: The Horizontal Threads

The horizontal threads in the fabric of the ship's sails represent three leading-edge ideas that provide a strong theoretical base for Powerful Student Care: (1) an ethic of hospitality (Ruitenberg, 2015), (2) cultural humility (Foronda et al., 2016), and (3) equity through belonging and dignity (Cobb & Krownapple, 2019) (see Figure 3.1).

FIGURE 3.1

Bodies of Knowledge: The Fabric of Our Sails

An Ethic of Hospitality	Pedagogies for Deep, Joy-Filled Learning		Equity, Dignity, Belonging
	Antiracist and Antibias Practices	Cultural Humility	Antiracist and Antibias Practices
An Ethic of Hospitality	Culturally Responsive and Sustaining Practices		Equity, Dignity, Belonging
	Empowerment Practices	Cultural Humility	Empowerment Practices
An Ethic of Hospitality	Student Engagement, Voice, and Aspirations		Equity, Dignity, Belonging
	Social-Emotional Learning	Cultural Humility	Social-Emotional Learning
An Ethic of Hospitality	Resiliency-Building Practices		Equity, Dignity, Belonging
	Disrupting Poverty	Cultural Humility	Disrupting Poverty
An Ethic of Hospitality	Trauma-Informed Practices		Equity, Dignity, Belonging

An Ethic of Hospitality

An ethic of hospitality provides a theoretical grounding for the provision of Powerful Student Care. This ethic is not about following a set of principles or rules, but rather serves as a guide for decision making and action in educational settings.

Claudia Ruitenberg (2015) is the educational philosopher who offers this fresh, compelling philosophy of education. To educate, she asserts, is to unlock worlds of past knowledge for students while leaving space for each student to offer newness to these worlds. "The ethic is all about… giving place to a guest" (p. 14). Hospitality, Ruitenberg suggests, "is a gift given by a host [educator] who is aware of her or his indebtedness to the guest" (p. 14). In other words, only because the guest (student) comes to the threshold are we, as educators, given the opportunity to host.

Ruitenberg's philosophy resembles an instructional approach to which Kathleen was introduced years ago: Quantum teaching. As the authors of the book *Quantum Teaching* note,

> In order for you to earn the right to teach, you must first build authentic bridges into your students' lives. A teaching credential or a document stating you can teach or train merely states you have the authority to teach. It doesn't mean you have the right to teach. Teaching someone is an earned right and is granted by the student, not by the state Department of Education. (Deporter et al., 1999, p. 6)

When applied to education, this ethic departs from two prevailing notions of hospitality. First, if we host guests in our home, they will tend to reciprocate in their home; however, Ruitenberg (2015) speaks of hospitality not simply as a gift, but as one that is given unconditionally, without the expectation that students will reciprocate. The second prevailing notion of hospitality is that the host has power over the guest, whereas Ruitenberg argues for the host to give power over to the guest (Ruitenberg, 2015). In making these moves, educators, as hosts, are asked to wrestle with three tensions: (1) the need to welcome students who cannot be known in advance; (2) the need to "protect the home" (school or classroom) while also providing a place that is "surrendered" to the guest (centering, empowering, and granting some level of autonomy to students); and (3) the need to provide hospitality without the expectation of reciprocity (unconditional welcome and belonging) (Ruitenberg, 2018).

As an educational philosophy, an ethic of hospitality is quite new to preK–12 education. We are only now beginning to ascertain what it could mean for schooling, even as Ruitenberg (2018) herself acknowledges the challenges it poses to educators. She asserts, "The current conditions of mass schooling in which demand after demand is piled on teachers make it difficult to practice an ethic of hospitality" (p. 42). Still, she says, the demand of this ethic is not that we achieve it, but that we continue to try "to do better in the tension between self-preservation and self-sacrifice, between unconditional gift and conditional exchange," to ensure each student experiences a hospitable place to learn and grow (p. 41). Ruitenberg calls us to see and grapple with the ways in which an ethic of hospitality "pulls at everyday schooling practices, [because] an education that does not maintain a reference to the principle of unconditional hospitality loses its reference to justice" (p. 42). We think about the tenets of Powerful Student Care in the same way—as pulling at everyday schooling practices and structures that have not served all students equally well.

Cultural Humility

Cultural humility is defined as "a lifelong process of self-reflection and self-critique whereby the individual not only learns about another's culture, but one also starts with an examination of her/his own beliefs and cultural identities" (National Institutes of Health, cited in Sufrin, 2019). It has also been described as the "ability to maintain an interpersonal stance that is other-oriented in relation to the aspects of cultural identity that are most important to that [person]" (Hook et al., cited in Waters & Asbill, 2013, p. 2). In other words, to practice cultural humility is to be open to learning about others' cultural identities in the manner in which they recognize them, particularly when they are different from our own.

The concept of cultural humility was first introduced by two physicians, Melanie Tervalon and Jann Murray-Garcia, in a 1998 article published in the *Journal of Health Care for the Poor and Underserved* and is characterized by three principles:

1. A lifelong commitment to self-reflection and critique;
2. Recognizing and "fixing" power imbalances (e.g., understanding that both the caregiver and the client possess knowledge that is valuable to the provision of care); and
3. Working at the institutional level with others to advocate for improvements in policies and practices.

The concept of cultural humility has been used in therapeutic professions such as nursing and social work for 30 years. Training in cultural humility is "central to a high standard of patient and community care" in these fields (Hannon & Amidon, 2020).

In the field of education, Chayla Rutledge Slaton (2020) argues that an emerging shift is occurring from a focus on cultural competency to one on cultural humility. Foronda and colleagues (2016) argue that cultural humility requires a greater shift in "perspective and way of life" than does cultural competency, as it is not only about gaining knowledge and skills, but also understanding one's "way of being" in the world (p. 214):

> In a multicultural world where power imbalances exist, cultural humility is a process of openness, self-awareness, being egoless, and incorporating self-reflection and critique after willingly interacting with diverse individuals. The results of achieving cultural humility are mutual empowerment, respect, partnership, optimal care, and life-long learning. (p. 213)

Slaton (2020) found that students who perceive their teachers as acting from a disposition of cultural humility form stronger working alliances with them, and that this is especially true when students report low feelings of school belongingness. The research of Tinkler and Tinkler (2016) shows that teachers who assume a culturally humble disposition tend to listen to students' life stories and consider how they shaped their students' identities. Through listening and dialogue, these teachers discover students' strengths, which in turn challenge their formerly held deficit perspectives. As one teacher explained,

" 'Because those assumptions can lead you to beliefs about people that aren't accurate… and you come to understand their background in a different way, it helps you to meet their needs academically' " (p. 199).

Cultural humility is a process of continually gaining a deeper understanding of cultural differences. "It reflects an other-oriented stance that is marked by openness, curiosity, lack of arrogance, and genuine desire to understand clients' cultural identities" (Hook et al., cited in Slaton, 2020, pp. 73–74). The more we practice cultural humility, the more we recognize how challenging it is to truly understand another person's cultural identity, reinforcing the need for humility (Yeager & Bauer-Wu, 2013). Openness, self-awareness, self-reflection, and a willingness to both give and receive critique help ensure optimal powerful care for our students and ourselves.

Cultural humility is vital to enacting the five tenets. Not only does it support us in enacting an ethic of hospitality, but it also exemplifies the disposition necessary for the third major strand in the fabric of our sails: understanding the link between equity, dignity, and belonging.

Equity Through Belonging and Dignity

In their book *Belonging Through a Culture of Dignity: The Keys to Successful Equity Implementation*, Cobb and Krownapple (2019) ask whether we as educators have "granted ourselves permission to create classrooms, schools, and district cultures where we can and do disregard the inherent value and worth of certain people" (p. 13). Claiming most equity initiatives don't "work," they describe well-intentioned but failed efforts as part of "the Dysfunctional Cycle of Equity Work." As they explain,

> The foundational reason [equity initiatives fail] is the non-inclusive and non-welcoming (certain students, families, or staff members don't belong) climate that is inherent in our school system… [such] unwelcoming environments where certain people do not belong are part of the legacy we've inherited as educators in this country. (p. 13)

According to the authors, efforts to ensure equity are too often singularly focused on "diversity," the meaning of which varies. Rather than increasing or valuing diversity, Cobb and Krownapple (2019) write, realizing equity necessitates a goal of inclusion and belonging:

> Inclusion is engagement within a community where the equal worth and inherent dignity of each person is honored. An inclusive community promotes and sustains a sense of belonging; it affirms the talents, beliefs, backgrounds, and ways of living of its members. (p. 33)

These scholars strongly advocate for "dust[ing] off our knowledge of Maslow" and prioritizing the "belonging gap" (pp. 42, 45). To ensure equity, it is necessary to attend not just to "the belonging gap" but also to "the opportunity gap," which is primarily about unequal access to a quality education. Acknowledging that students of color and those living in poverty have historically been denied access to the same learning opportunities provided to their white and affluent peers, Cobb and Krownapple point to research that demonstrates "belonging matters just as much" as access. "Access and belonging are two sides of the same coin," they write. "Belonging is the step before achievement. Indeed, achievement is built on belonging" (pp. 42, 45).

According to Cobb and Krownapple, school "culture is the strategy" to ensure that students experience both "belonging and access" (p. 89). They define culture as "the way we do things around here" and climate as the way students experience the culture (p. 68). They suggest equity is about transforming school cultures into cultures of inclusion.

Such cultures are not created by happenstance. "Inclusion is about partnering with the people we are serving and changing the culture so those we serve experience access and unconditional belonging," Cobb and Krownapple write. "That's a different paradigm than expecting people to change themselves in order to fit in" (p. 86). An inclusive, welcoming school culture and climate "must be based on a culture of dignity. Dignity is how we do belonging and inclusion" (p. 89).

Dignity is different from respect. Respect must be granted. Respect is an admiration that must be earned, and it can be lost. By contrast, dignity cannot be lost because it is a birthright. Cobb and Krownapple contend that educators must fully understand this distinction. They turn to the definitions of dignity offered by Donna

Hicks (2011), a conflict resolution specialist at Harvard University, who defines it as "equal human value and worth" and also as "an internal state of peace that comes with the recognition and acceptance of the value and vulnerability of all living things" (quoted in Cobb & Krownapple, 2019, p. 96).

It's the second part of Hicks's definition that Cobb and Krownapple find especially important. "Even though we're equally valuable," they explain, "we're not all equally vulnerable at all times" (p. 96). Emphasizing the need for educators to "fully understand this concept and begin to see dignity as a moral imperative" (p. 97), they call on us to develop a "dignity-consciousness." We build belonging by honoring our students' dignity. Moreover, "dignity is the precursor to cultural responsiveness and any other equity methodology ever conceived— past, present, or future" (p. 106).

The Fabric of Our Sails: The Vertical Threads

Woven between the horizontal threads in the fabric of our sails are vertical threads that symbolize additional research- and practice-based bodies of knowledge that support educators in realizing Powerful Student Care. This knowledge base includes what we know about

- Responding to trauma;
- Disrupting the adverse impact of poverty on learning;
- Building resiliency in students;
- Integrating social and emotional learning with academic learning;
- Engaging and empowering students by giving them voice and connecting their learning to their aspirations;
- Providing a culturally responsive and sustaining learning environment;
- Engaging in antibias and antiracist work; and
- Employing curricular and instructional designs that promote deep, joy-filled learning.

Look again at Figure 3.1 (p. 33) to see how the horizontal and vertical threads fit together to form the strong weave of the sails of the PSC *Encounter*. Together, these threads form the way of knowing that is Powerful Student Care. In the next chapter, we survey the PSC *Encounter*'s safety devices as we connect our way of being and our way of knowing to our way of thinking.

4

A Way of Thinking

If you want to awaken all of humanity, awaken all of yourself.

—Lao Tzu

Like any maritime vessel, the PSC *Encounter* comes with an inventory of safety features that can save lives. Those that are most visible to our passengers include lifeboats, life jackets, and flotation devices. PSC captains use these items to ensure that each student is experiencing the tenets of community. They represent a disciplined way of thinking that connects the five tenets of community, the expertise and intro-spective capacity of the educator, and the needs and interests of each student.

The Contemplative Practice as a Habit of Mind

The Contemplative Practice is a habit of mind that includes inquiry, analysis, and action. When we think of the word *contemplative*, several ideas come to mind:

- To think seriously or to plan;
- To consider, to foresee, to intend, or to deliberate;
- To design, to observe, or to speculate; and
- To study, to aspire to, to muse over, to reflect upon, to weigh, or to critique.

We all know what these words mean, and many of us have used them as we taught higher-order thinking skills or gauged lessons against the Depth of Knowledge continuum or Bloom's taxonomy. Thinking isn't new to educators; we make hundreds of decisions every single day. These decisions regularly come in rapid succession, and often we have little time to think them through. Because we have been asked to make so many decisions, our current habits of mind may focus on giving answers rather than on asking questions. In her work coaching and consulting with teachers over the years, Kathleen has often helped teachers move from being a "good answerer" to being a "good questioner."

You might be thinking, "I don't have time to ask questions; I have to have answers." Unfortunately, this way of thinking leads us to waste a lot of time pursuing solution after solution.

Those who have solved some of the world's most vexing problems understand the power of being a good questioner. The ability to ask questions is one of the things that differentiates humans from other animals. We are driven to ask questions because we are aware of what we do not know. As Warren Berger (2014) notes, this awareness separates "the smart and curious" from those who are not comfortable with acknowledging their lack of knowledge or those who simply don't care (p. 16).

As a habit of mind, questioning is power. Dan Rothstein and Luz Santana established the Right Question Institute (www.right question.org), a nonprofit organization dedicated to helping teachers (and others) develop their own and their students' questioning skills. Rothstein believes "questions have an 'unlocking' effect in people's mind" (cited in Berger, 2014, p. 16). Steve Quatrano, also with the Right Question Institute, says that "forming questions helps us to 'organize our thinking around what we don't know'" (cited in Berger, 2014, p. 16).

In his 2014 book *A More Beautiful Question: The Power of Inquiry to Spark Breakthrough Ideas,* Berger dedicates an entire chapter to the reasons we stop asking questions as we get older. He points to studies that demonstrate preschoolers ask, on average, 100 questions a day, but by middle school, most kids have stopped asking questions. Berger ponders:

To the extent school is like a factory, students who inquire about "the way things are" could be seen as insubordinate. It raises, at least in my mind, a question that may seem extreme: If schools were built on a factory model, were they actually designed to squelch questions? (p. 48)

Too much of contemporary schooling squelches inquiry not only in students but also in educators. The anti-questioning culture that is seemingly baked into the system is coupled with information overload: "Without a filtering device, we can't separate what's relevant or reliable from what is not" (Berger, 2014, p. 25).

David Cooperrider, developer of the popular theory of appreciative inquiry, notes that "we all live in the world our questions create" (cited in Berger, 2014, p. 18). In the context of Powerful Student Care, the habit of asking questions focuses on trying to understand what each student experiences. The tenets of community guide us to ask questions that can shape the world we co-create with our students. Do our students feel safe? Do they feel welcomed? Do they have a voice? Do they feel supported in their aspirations? Do they feel valued? When they struggle, what causes the struggle? How do their life experiences and identity shape how they see and experience community? To what degree do they believe they are both distinctive and irreplaceable? Asking and answering such questions has implications for the actions we take on behalf of each student.

Because PSC is a way of being, a way of knowing, *and* a way of thinking, it resists being added to a to-do list. In our everyday interactions with colleagues, students, and families, we define the Contemplative Practice as the deliberate study and observation to predict, plan for, and respond to the ever-changing needs of each of our children (Chandler, 2019).

The Contemplative Practice as the PSC *Encounter*'s Life Preserver

As you read through the three phases of the Contemplative Practice in this section, you will notice the importance of surfacing, interrogating, and redefining our mental models. In *The Fifth Discipline*, Peter

Senge (1990/2006) defines models as "deeply ingrained assumptions, generalizations, or even pictures or images that influence how we understand the world and how we take action. Very often we are not consciously aware of our mental models or the effects they have on our behavior" (p. 8). Surfacing, interrogating, and defining these mental models is fundamental to the Contemplative Practice.

When we reflect upon and critique our mental models, we are more likely to be effective in our roles because we are more aware of our biases and assumptions, resulting in only a small gap between our espoused and our unspoken rationales for action (Argyris & Schön, 1974). Implicit bias is a good case in point: When we are aware of and challenge the implicit bias that is part of our mental models, we can better meet the needs of each student.

Educators who employ the Contemplative Practice confront and respond to their mental models and to the institutional barriers that reproduce the marginalization and oppression of some groups of students, choosing always to respond to each student as though they are distinctive and irreplaceable (Chandler & Budge, 2020).

There are three phases to the Contemplative Practice: Predict, Plan For, and Respond (see Figure 4.1). On one level, the Contemplative Practice focuses on student needs and how we respond to them; on another level, the focus is on introspection, reflection, and metacognition.

Phase One: Predict

In the Predict phase, we investigate and interpret all available information to understand student needs as best we can. We ask questions that will likely require us to observe students in class, review their work, and watch as they interact with peers. We might talk to other adults who interact with these students at the school. Most important, we will engage in direct conversations with students to understand what they are feeling and experiencing in school. At the same time, we surface and question our own mental models related to students' needs and interests, our classroom communities of difference, and our skills and knowledge for extending Powerful Student Care.

FIGURE 4.1

The Three Phases of Contemplative Practice

Leverage Strengths to Pinpoint Most Effective Means

Ways of Being, Ways of Knowing, Ways of Thinking

Investigate and Interpret Available Information

Questions About My Students, Me, and My Actions

Questions to Surface, Interrogate, and Define My Mental Models

Position Thinking into Responsive Action

Questions About My Plan and Its Results

Questions to Resurface, Reinterrogate, and Redefine My Mental Models

PLAN FOR

PREDICT

RESPOND

Phase Two: Plan For

In the Plan For phase, we draw upon our ways of knowing, reflecting on the foundational philosophy of Powerful Student Care: extending hospitality as an unconditional gift through cultural humility and ensuring equity through dignity and belonging. We draw upon the other bodies of knowledge—the vertical strands of our sails—to pinpoint the most effective ways to meet students' needs and fulfill their interests. We leverage our strengths and our ways of knowing to select and utilize the right navigational instruments to bring our students to each port of call. We also ask ourselves why we think our intended course of action is most effective and how it challenges or aligns with our existing mental models.

Phase Three: Respond

Finally, in the Respond phase, we move from inquiry to action. We determine when we will act, what we need to get ready to act, and how we will document the execution and impact of our plan. As we understand the impact of our actions on students' experiences, we use that knowledge to determine where to begin the cycle of the Contemplative Practice again. We also think about our own learning and growth and whether and to what degree our new learning has altered our mental models. Once we understand that our mental models can change because we've learned something we didn't know before, we realize there is always more to learn. In addition to being a continuous habit of mind, the Contemplative Practice presents a continual growth process for our mental models.

The Contemplative Practice in Action

Figure 4.2 summarizes each phase of the Contemplative Practice and provides questions to foster a spirit of inquiry and develop the habit of mind necessary to enact Powerful Student Care. These questions can guide your thinking through the three phases of Contemplative Practice. The list of questions offered is not meant to be exhaustive, nor is it necessary to answer each question every time you engage in the Contemplative Practice. In subsequent chapters, we provide additional questions aligned to each of the tenets of Powerful Student Care to provide additional guidance.

FIGURE 4.2

The Contemplative Practice: Spirit of Inquiry

Predict
Investigate and Interpret Available Information

Preparing for the provision of Powerful Student Care to each student, I begin by investigating and interpreting available information, asking...

Questions About My Students	• Who is each student?
	  – What aspirations does each hold?
	  – How does each self-identify?
	  – What identities (e.g., cultural, gender, religious, geo-graphic, sexual, class-based) does each student bring with them?
	  – How does each student view themselves as a learner?
	  – What strengths does each student possess?

Questions About Me and My Actions	• What are my strengths? • What actions have I taken to extend the tenets of community to each student to date? • What actions have I taken to withhold the tenets of community from any student to date? • How, if at all, am I responding to barriers I am facing in extending the tenets of community to each student?
Questions to Surface and Interrogate and Define My Mental Models	• What might it mean to walk in each of my students' shoes? • What are my current beliefs about extending the tenets of community to each student? • Upon what are these beliefs based? • What data, if any, disconfirms my beliefs? • How might my beliefs and biases be creating barriers to extending the tenets of community to each student?

Plan For
Leverage Strengths to Pinpoint Most Effective Means

Based on what I know about each student, myself, and the tenets of community, I develop a plan for leveraging strengths and pinpointing the most effective means for the provision of Powerful Student Care, asking...

Questions About Ways of Being	• Given what I know about my strengths and the strengths of my students, what navigational instruments (Figure 2.1, p. 30) will I use and how will I use them to extend the five tenets of community to each student and among students?

(continued)

FIGURE 4.2

The Contemplative Practice: Spirit of Inquiry—(*continued*)

Plan For—(*continued*)	
Leverage Strengths to Pinpoint Most Effective Means	
Questions About Ways of Knowing	• How will I use the knowledge I have gained related to an ethic of hospitality, cultural humility, and equity through dignity and belonging to extend the tenets of community to each student? • How will I use the knowledge I possess and other expertise (Figure 3.1, p. 33) I hold to extend the tenets of community to each student?
Questions About Ways of Thinking	• How will I use questions from each phase of the Contemplative Practice to ensure each student experiences each of the tenets of community? • How effectively have I surfaced my mental models to extend the tenets of community to each student? • What is my plan of action? • Why do I believe it is the best course of action?
Respond	
Turn Thinking into Responsive Action	
Having selected the most effective means for providing Powerful Student Care to each student, I position my thinking into responsive action, asking...	
Questions About My Plan	• When am I going to put my plan into action? • What do I need to do to get ready to execute my plan? • What help do I need and from whom can I get that help? • What resources do I need and how will I acquire those resources? • How do I document my plan's impact as I execute my plan?
Questions About the Results of My Plan	• What worked and how did I know? • What did not work and how did I know? • What will I do more, differently, or better next time? • How will I continue to increase my capacity to extend the tenets of community to each student?
Questions to Resurface, Reinterrogate, and Redefine My Mental Models	• What were my mental models (images, assumptions, beliefs) related to extending the five tenets of community to each student before I began the work of doing so? • How, if at all, were my mental models challenged in the process of doing the work? • How, if at all, were my mental models changed? • How, if at all, were these changes beneficial?

As we move to Level 2, we will shift our focus from theory to practice. We settle aboard the PSC *Encounter* and conduct a learning tour, including a detailed investigation of each port of call on our map as we sail toward The Harbor. As we briefly disembark at each port, you will be introduced to one of our PSC captains, all of whom are making their way toward The Harbor with their students. You will have the opportunity to observe a brief segment of their journey and witness the captains using their expertise, intellect, and humanity in the process of navigating their own PSC ships. You will observe these individuals as they use the three phases of the Contemplative Practice to create and execute an action plan intended to ensure that each of their amazing students experiences the tenets of community.

~~~~~~~~~~~~~~~~~~~~~

A Learning Tour
of Five Ports of Call

5

Each Student Is
Welcomed and Valued

You must never be fearful about what you are doing when it is the right thing.

—Rosa Parks

Welcome aboard the Institute's sailing vessel, the PSC *Encounter*. Once we set sail, we'll use our travel time to learn about the first two tenets of community, which are the first two ports of call on the journey to The Harbor. Using our map as a guide (see Figure 5.1, p. 54), we will first deeply explore the meaning and research base for the first two tenets of community: *each student is welcomed to be a part of our community* and *each student is a valued member of our community*. By the end of this chapter, we hope you will have a solid understanding of these two tenets. Let's get started.

FIGURE 5.1

The Map to The Harbor: The First Two Ports of Call

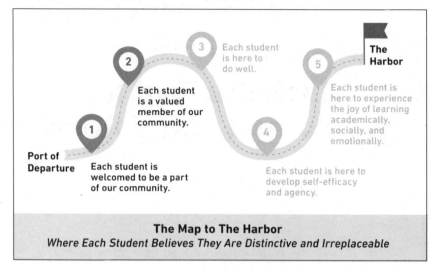

2

3 Each student
is here to
do well.

Each student
is a valued
member of our
community.

**The
Harbor**

5

1

Each student is
here to experience
the joy of learning
academically,
socially, and
emotionally.

**Port of
Departure**

Each student is
welcomed to be a part
of our community.

4

Each student is here to
develop self-efficacy
and agency.

The Map to The Harbor
Where Each Student Believes They Are Distinctive and Irreplaceable

What Does It Mean to Welcome and to Value Each Student?

Let's begin by focusing on what it means for a student to feel welcomed. Give yourself some time right now to study Figure 5.2.

Welcoming each student—think about it. To what degree have we in education even thought that "feeling welcome" matters? After all, children are compelled to be in school. We didn't "invite" them. And for far too many, schools are not hospitable places.

In her book *Wounded by School: Recapturing the Joy in Learning and Standing Up to Old School Culture* (2009), educational consultant Kirsten Olson describes the ways in which schools wound students. She didn't begin her research looking for this data; rather, she was seeking to understand the "emotional and psychological experiences" of highly engaged learners to better understand how they "become avid and self-confident, and what those peak moments of learning were actually like from an emotional and affective point of view" (p. 3).

FIGURE 5.2

Defining Welcoming

The Tenet	What It Means	What We Say Directly to Students	What We Want Students to Say Directly to Us
Each student is welcomed to be part of our community.	**If** we unconditionally extend welcome to each student by embracing each student's multidimensional identity as co-creators of a community of difference... **Then** each student feels appreciated, validated, respected, included, supported, and treated equitably, all of which contribute to the fulfillment of the innate human need to belong.	"We want you to feel you belong here."	"I am home. I belong. I have friends. I feel connected to the people here. I know people care for me and I care for them."

The individuals Olson interviewed included a university professor, a venture capitalist, and a gifted writer. They were all successful by conventional standards. Yet nearly as soon as Olson started her interviews, they began to talk about their "educational wounding." Patterns across interviews soon emerged to reveal common educational practices that had been sources of "laceration and rupture" in the learning and in the souls of these one-time students (p. 4). Olson offers the following list of the sorts of wounds she discerned in her study:

- "Everyday" losses of pleasure in learning
- Belief that we are not smart, not competent in learning
- Belief that our abilities are fixed, and cannot be improved with effort, coaching intervention, or self-understanding
- Belief that we are "just average" in ways that feel diminishing
- Painful, burning memories of shaming experiences in school that produce generalized anxiety and shut us down
- Chronic, habitual anger toward teachers, and those in authority due to past experiences of injustice, not being "seen" in school

- Belief that we are intellectually or cognitively "less than" due to past experiences in school
- Low appetite for risk taking intellectually, wanting to be right or "just get the assignment done"
- Overattachment to "right" answers, correctness
- Tendency to classify others, and ourselves into dualistic, diminishing "smart/dumb," "artistic/not artistic" categories
- Unprocessed, powerful feelings about education and learning that we become aware of as adults, in our interaction with our children or students in school (p. 19)

Powerful Student Care could serve as a healing balm for many, if not most, of these wounds, and welcoming each student to our classroom community is the first step toward helping them develop a sense of belonging.

What Does It Mean to Be Welcomed?

In the context of Powerful Student Care, we welcome students into a community of difference, a place where they become *of* the community as co-creators, experiencing belonging and a sense of community. Recall the three horizontal strands in the fabric of the PSC *Encounter*'s sails: an ethic of hospitality, cultural humility, and equity through dignity and belonging. These bodies of knowledge inform each of the five PSC tenets, including what it means to welcome.

In welcoming students to our co-created community, an ethos of hospitality informs our actions and our dispositions. This ethos "is about the guest... the position of the host is radically de-centered" (Ruitenberg, 2015, p. 14). We don't welcome students because we are virtuous people, but because it is our responsibility. Ruitenberg says this responsibility comes with "having access to the world" [the world of knowledge and traditions]—a world that students both inherit and shape (p. 15). Central to this ethos "is the idea that those who already inhabit the world don't own it and that it is a general responsibility to share the world one happens to inhabit" (p. 16):

[W]hile perhaps the most common host-guest relation is that between teacher and student, the student would not be locked into the position of guest; the point of unlocking the world, of welcoming students to traditions and worlds is that the students are able to take place in them and, in turn, host others. Students then act as hosts also toward other students. (p. 26)

An ethic of hospitality also requires educators to be open to the "arrival of something and someone we cannot foresee" and to construct the educative experience "in such a way as to leave space for those students and those ideas that may arrive" (Ruitenberg, 2015, p. 30):

This may seem like an absurd demand: if they may (or may not) arrive, how do we know who or what they are and *what kind* of space we should leave for them. Indeed, we cannot know who or what may arrive in our classrooms... the only questions we can therefore ask are: Does what I am about to do leave a possibility for my assumptions about knowledge and teaching and learning to be upset by a new arrival? Does it close down a space for future questioning or questioners? (p. 30)

Our ability to co-create the educative experience with our students is aided by our practice of cultural humility, which asks us to recognize that both the teacher and the student possess knowledge and perspective that are valuable to the learning process. Moreover, assuming a culturally humble stance makes us more receptive to considering what each student brings to the table when we commit to self-reflection and critique.

What Do We Intend Students to Experience When They Are Welcomed?

We intend each student to experience belonging when they are welcomed into our community. Scholars define *belonging* as feeling appreciated, validated, accepted, respected, included, supported, and treated fairly (Barron & Kinney, 2021; Cobb & Krownapple, 2019). Communities that sustain a sense of belonging are places where "the equal worth and dignity of each person is honored" (Cobb & Krown-apple, 2019, p. 33).

The need to belong is hardwired in humans. As children's author Phoebe Stone (2011/2012) says, "Not belonging is a terrible feeling; it feels awkward and it hurts; as if you were wearing someone else's shoes" (p. 90). Decades of research show that "a host of positive personal, social, and academic benefits" (Barron & Kinney, 2021, p. 2) spring from a sense of belonging, including enhancements or increases to the following:

- Pro-social classroom behavior
- Attendance rates
- Self-esteem
- Self-confidence
- Self-belief
- Optimism
- Positive peer relationships
- Classroom engagement
- Focus on academic tasks
- Academic achievement
- School satisfaction
- Positive attitudes toward schooling and learning
- Skills of self-management
- Resilience to deal with crises
- Buffer against effects of a negative home environment (Barron & Kinney, 2021, pp. 2–3)

Children and youth who feel they belong "aren't worried and distracted about being treated as a stereotype or a thin slice of their multidimensional identities. Instead, they are confident that they are seen as a human being, a person of value" (p. 43)—in other words, as distinctive and irreplaceable.

What Does It Mean to Be Valued?

We ask you to pause at this point to read and reflect upon the information in Figure 5.3. Experiencing belonging begins with the knowledge that one is welcomed and is reinforced by the confidence that one is valued. The Quaglia Institute for School Voice and Aspirations (2020) notes that "self-worth begins when we experience a sense of Belonging. We feel like we are part of the school community while being recognized and appreciated for our uniqueness" (para. 5).

FIGURE 5.3

Defining Valuing

The Tenet	What It Means	What We Say Directly to Students	What We Want Students to Say Directly to Us
Each student is a valued member of our community.	**If** we categorically recognize the value of each student by affirming their inherent dignity (i.e., equal worth) as a human being through the creation of dignity-conscious relationships in an environment free of the negative role of stereotyping... **Then** each student feels sufficient safety and freedom to explore their developing sense of selfhood, experiences a deep and abiding sense of self-worth, and knows they have a seat at the table.	"We can't be as good as we are together without you."	"You care about what I have to say. I have a seat at the table, and I am heard. I can be who I am. I can become who I am."

Organizational psychologists Marian Iszatt-White and Kate Mackenzie-Davey (2003) define feeling valued as a "positive response arising from confirmation of an individual's possession of qualities on which worth or desirability depends" (p. 228). In the context of Powerful Student Care, students are valued simply because they are worthy of being valued as human beings. Cobb and Krownapple (2019) use the word *dignity* "to communicate the innate, *equal worth*" of each human being:

> Dignity is a noun with roots in Latin: "dignus" meaning "worthy."
> … Dignity is our common heritage and birth right as human beings.
> … Every person has dignity…. According to common definitions
> dignity is the state or quality of being worthy to belong…. Dignity
> stands above differences. (p. 95)

We uphold our students' dignity first and foremost through relationships. Cobb and Krownapple (2019) contend that the "quality of the teacher-student relationship is defined by the degree to which dignity is honored within that relationship." Dignity, they explain, "is the way to nurture belonging" (p. 104).

Dr. Donna Hicks (2018), international affairs and conflict resolution specialist at Harvard University, has developed a "Dignity Model" that can help us understand how to safeguard our students' dignity in our relationships with them. Her model includes the following 10 elements of dignity:

1. **Acceptance of Identity:** Give people the freedom to express their authentic selves without judgment.
2. **Recognition:** Validate people.
3. **Acknowledgment:** Respond to people's concerns.
4. **Inclusion:** Welcome others and make them feel they belong.
5. **Safety:** Put people at ease physically and psychologically.
6. **Fairness:** Treat people justly.
7. **Independence:** Empower people's agency.
8. **Understanding:** Actively listen to others' perspectives.
9. **Benefit of the Doubt:** Extend trust to others.
10. **Accountability:** Take responsibility for your actions and apologize for causing harm.

Educators should recognize and nurture students' multidimensional identities and their unique contributions to our community. In *Cultivating Genius: An Equity Framework for Culturally and Historically Responsive Literacy* (2020), Gholdy Muhammad tells us that identity "was one of the first things to be stripped from enslaved Africans, thus it became key for people of color to know themselves so they could tell their own stories. Consequently, identity was also one of the first areas we sought to reclaim" (p. 64). Muhammad defines identity as a collection of "notions of who we are, who others say we are (in both positive and negative ways), and whom we desire to be." It represents

> a complex and dynamic dance among the three toward identity development for both children and adults throughout our lives. Our identities (both cultural and others) are continually being (re)defined and revised.... [And], youth need opportunities in school to explore multiple facets of selfhood, but also to learn about the identities of others who may differ. (p. 67)

Valuing students, then, is about safeguarding their dignity through dignity-conscious relationships and co-creating a place where they can learn who they are and who they can become.

What Do We Intend Students to Experience When They Are Valued?

Our intention is for each student to feel a deep and abiding sense of self-worth through belonging that stems from being unconditionally welcomed and knowing they are valued for the distinctive and irreplaceable human being they are. We want students to feel sufficient safety and freedom to explore their developing sense of selfhood and to link their learning to their aspirations. In this way, we support them in writing their own story. Alexs Pate (2020), author of *The Innocent Classroom,* describes this sort of experience as "innocence":

> Innocence is the condition that results from the reduction, minimization, neutralization or elimination of the guilt that develops from stereotypes and popular negative narrative and iconography.... Innocence is an immeasurably beautiful and important gift that all teachers can give their students. When children believe what they are being taught can have a positive impact on their lives and that they deserve the lessons they are being taught, and when they can walk the halls of a school or enter a classroom without the weight of the negative expectations, they will respond more positively to the academic challenges put before them. (p. 10)

We want students to feel increasingly confident in their seat at the table when we invite them to co-create their educative experience. As best-selling author Roxane Gay said on the podcast *Seat at the Table,* "A seat at the table means that you are a part of the conversation" (St-Victor & Racicot, 2020). In the realization of Powerful Student Care, students know they have a voice. They know they are heard.

Barriers to Welcoming and Valuing

Barriers to welcoming and valuing each student are as significant as the stakes are high. "When we sense that somebody else sees us with less value, we worry that we will be kicked out of our protective group, and some predator will come and eat us," writes Joseph Shrand (2020). Feeling like we don't belong results in a host of negative consequences such as emotional distress, anger and frustration, erosion of self-worth, distraction from learning tasks, difficulty with self-management, and susceptibility to self-defeating behavior (Barron & Kinney, 2021).

Though certain barriers to children feeling welcomed and valued are beyond the control of individual educators, one of the most significant barriers is exclusively within our sphere of influence—namely, our willingness to deeply know our students and marshal the courage to confront our mental models. When we know our students well and are engaged in interrogating our mental models, we are better prepared to avoid three phenomena that can get in our way: stereotyping and stereotype threat, othering, and violations to dignity.

Stereotyping and Stereotype Threat

Children and youth who have been historically excluded and marginalized suffer a disproportionate impact when they do not experience belonging (Cobb & Krownapple, 2019). As Pate (2020) reminds us, the "the damage that negative stereotyping does to our children is massive and wide-ranging" (p. 3). He explains:

When our children were born, they were free. Undamaged. They open their eyes to a horizon with no limits.... Unfortunately, the world had a plan for them.... Children of color [and other margin-alized children] are being held in virtual bondage to the negative stereotypes that our culture has developed and perpetuated about them....For many children these stereotypes actually become a script that influences their behavior and inhibits their ability to be engaged learners. (p. 3)

Decades of research support Pate's claim. Stereotype threat has a devastating impact on students and student achievement. Steele and Aronson (1995), who coined the term *stereotype threat*, found that students often underachieve, even though they are motivated to succeed, when they are conscious of their stigmatized identities in relation to the task they are asked to perform. For example, they found that females underperform on math and science tests when they are conscious of stereotypes related to gender and performance on such tests. Likewise, people of color whose racial identities are stigmatized by stereotypes related to intelligence have been found to underperform on tests purported to measure intelligence. John Hattie (2019) has calculated that the adverse impact on achievement due to stereotype threat is equal to a full 83 percent of one year's growth.

Pate (2020) describes this deleterious effect of stereotypes as pro-ducing "guilt," which he defines as *"the absence of innocence"* (p. 25):

This guilt imbues children with a sense that they have done some-thing wrong before they've actually done it. It's no surprise, then, that guilt triggers cynicism, anger, apathy, and a general sense of opposition to education. Our children get the sense that it doesn't really matter what they do or how they behave; the world will see them as guilty because that is the way the world sees them already. (p. 26)

Othering

Gholdy Muhammad (2020) often asks teachers to tell her about their students. "Sadly," she says, "I am usually flooded with negative responses and comments about perceived weaknesses of the students in their schools and classrooms" (p. 65). Teachers tell her, "My students aren't invested in their learning. My students can't read. My students aren't motivated" (p. 65). Although these teachers use the phrase "my students," she questions whether they would introduce their own children to her in the same pejorative manner. If not, she asks, "Why are we still 'othering' children" (p. 65)?

What *is* othering? According to Cobb and Krownapple (2019), othering is what prevents us from ensuring that each student feels belonging (p. 121). They define *othering* as the opposite of belonging and assert it is "an ancient instinct: that of tribalism; the 'us versus them' mentality; our innate hostility toward the unfamiliar; and the instinct to perceive and push back against those who are different than us." "We all do it," they claim (p. 121). Nonetheless, we can learn to identify the following four indicators of othering:

> Otherized: Viewed, treated, and made to seem *different* in a way that ostracizes, denigrates, reduces, and dehumanizes (labels, objectifies, animalizes, etc.). (Cobb & Krownapple, 2019, p. 122)

> Mistreated: Dealt with in a way that is unfair, unjust, and biased due to perceptions about your identity, group membership, conditions, circumstances, or cultural practices/norms. (Cobb & Krownapple, 2019, p. 123)

> Marginalized: Rejected and pushed to the edge of a group(s); put or kept in a position of limited significance, influence, and power; only able to gain access and belonging by changing or hiding important aspects of one's self. (Cobb & Krownapple, 2019, p. 124)

> Dismissed: Having your lived experience or expertise questioned, invalidated, and/or deemed insufficient. (Cobb & Krownapple, 2019, p. 125)

Put simply, when we engage in othering, we "see people as less than human" (Cobb & Krownapple, 2019, p. 121).

Violations to Dignity

"It's a natural human failing that when we feel our own dignity is vulnerable, we can be tempted to violate the dignity of others" (Cobb

& Krownapple, 2019, p. 126). Hicks (2011) offers 10 ways in which we tend to distort or fail to honor the dignity of ourselves or others:

1. **Taking the bait**—letting the bad behavior of others determine our own for the purpose of getting even
2. **Saving face**—lying to cover up or deceive others to prevent ourselves from looking bad in their eyes
3. **Shirking responsibility**—refusing to admit when we've made a mistake and shifting the blame onto someone else
4. **Seeking false dignity**—depending on others alone for validation of our worth
5. **Seeking false security**—remaining in relationships where our dignity is routinely violated
6. **Avoiding conflict**—allowing someone to violate our dignity without speaking up for ourselves
7. **Playing the victim**—claiming innocence in failed relationships
8. **Resisting feedback**—deflecting feedback about our individual blind spots
9. **Blaming or shaming others to deflect guilt**—placing the blame on others so as not to be exposed of wrongdoing
10. **Gossiping**—talking about people in a negative way in order to connect with others

Again, we all do these things. Because we have the need to belong, we are susceptible to them. For example, we acclimate to toxic school cultures, even when we know they are toxic, in order to belong. We blame students (or their families, or their economic circumstances, or their culture, or their race) when they fail to learn what we have attempted to teach them to deflect questions about our own competency. In this way, we shirk our responsibility to "go back to the drawing board" when students need two, three, four, or more chances to learn. When the data demonstrates that we disproportionately discipline boys of color, we deflect feedback about our blind spots because it doesn't fit our self-perception.

In providing Powerful Student Care, we confront these barriers in part through the practice of cultural humility (see Chapter 4). Educators who practice cultural humility strengthen the connection between themselves and their students. They listen to students' stories and the manner in which those narratives shape their identities. They affirm students' strengths, reject stereotypes, and challenge the deficit perspectives they once held (Tinkler & Tinkler, 2016).

Connecting the Contemplative Practice to the Tenets of Welcoming and Valuing

In Chapter 4, we defined the Contemplative Practice as a habit of mind that entails inquiry, analysis, and action. Questions focused on welcoming and valuing each student to consider in each phase of the Contemplative Practice are provided in Figure 5.4.

FIGURE 5.4

Contemplative Practice for Welcoming and Valuing

Predict	
Investigate and Interpret Available Information	
Preparing to welcome and value each student, I investigate and interpret available information, asking the following questions:	

Questions About My Students	• Who is each student?
	   – How does each student self-identify?
	   – Who has a strong sense of self-worth? Who doesn't?
	   – Who believes that their dignity (innate equal worth) as a human being is honored in my classroom? Who does not?
	
	• Who experiences physical, social, and emotional safety?
	   – Who has strong relationships with me that safeguard their dignity? Who doesn't?
	   – Who has strong relationships with their peers that safeguard their dignity? Who doesn't?
	   – Who experiences a community free of the negative impacts of stereotyping? Who doesn't?
	
	• How does each student co-create a sense of community?
	   – Who believes that their voice is heard? Who doesn't?
	   – Who believes they make unique contributions to our classroom? Who doesn't?
	   – Who feels confident in having a seat at the table? Who doesn't?

Questions About Me and My Actions	• What are my strengths in relationship to welcoming and valuing? • How do I know that what I've learned about my students' experiences is accurate? • What actions have I taken to honor each student's identity, safeguard their dignity, and enhance their self-worth? • What actions have I taken to develop strong relationships that safeguard student's dignity and ensure a community free of the negative impacts of stereotyping? • What actions have I taken to honor each student's voice and their unique contributions to co-creating our community of difference? • What actions have I taken that withhold the tenets of community from any students? • • What actions or inactions on my part may have been counterproductive, destructive, or threatening to each student's experience of welcoming and valuing? • How, if at all, am I responding to barriers I face welcoming and valuing each student?
Questions to Surface, Interrogate, and Define My Mental Models	• What might it mean to walk in each of my students' shoes? • What are my current beliefs about welcoming each student unconditionally? • What are my current beliefs about valuing each student's multidimensional identity? • What stereotypes or biases have I surfaced in myself about my students' multidimensional identities or inherent dignity as human beings? • Upon what are these beliefs or biases based? • What data, if any, disconfirms my beliefs or biases? • How might my beliefs and biases be creating barriers to welcoming and valuing each student?
Plan For Leverage Strengths to Pinpoint Most Effective Means	
Based on what I know about myself, each student, and the tenets of community, I develop a plan for leveraging my strengths and pinpointing the most effective means for providing Powerful Student Care, asking the following questions:	
Questions About Our Way of Being	• Given what I know about my strengths and the strengths of my students, what navigational instruments (see Figure 2.1, p. 30) will I use, and how will I use them to welcome and value each student?
Questions About Our Way of Knowing	• How will I use the knowledge I have gained related to an ethic of hospitality, cultural humility, and equity through dignity and belonging to welcome and value each student? • How will I use the knowledge I possess and other expertise I hold (see Figure 3.1, p. 33) to welcome and value each student?

(continued)

FIGURE 5.4

Contemplative Practice for Welcoming and Valuing—(*continued*)

Plan For	
Leverage Strengths to Pinpoint Most Effective Means—(*continued*)	
Questions About Our Way of Thinking	• How will I use questions from each phase of the Contemplative Practice to welcome and value each student? • How effectively have I surfaced my mental models to welcome and value each student? • What course of action do I plan to take? • Why do I believe this is the best course of action?
Respond	
Turn Thinking into Responsive Action	
Having selected the most effective means for welcoming and valuing each student, I turn my thinking into responsive action, asking the following questions:	
Questions About My Plan	• When am I going to put my plan into action? • What do I need to do to get ready to execute my plan? • What help do I need and from whom can I get that help? • What resources do I need and how will I acquire those resources? • How do I document my plan's impact as I execute it?
Questions About the Results of My Plan	• What worked, and how did I know it worked? • What didn't work, and how did I know it didn't work? • What will I do better next time? • How will I continue to increase my capacity to extend the tenets of community to each student?
Questions to Resurface, Reinterrogate, and Redefine My Mental Models	• What were my mental models (images, assumptions, beliefs) related to extending welcoming and belonging to each student before I began the work of doing so? • How, if at all, were my mental models challenged in the process of doing the work? • How, if at all, did my mental models change? • How, if at all, were these changes beneficial?

These questions focus our thinking so we can carefully analyze and better understand our students' experiences. Asking and answering these questions also prepares us to plan for and respond to students' needs and interests in a manner that is not solely based on our hunches. It is likely that we will use only some of the questions at any given time and that the answers to some questions may make us uncomfortable. Often, there's a disconnect between what we extend (that which we try to create, foster, or provide) and what our students actually feel and experience.

Having used our sailing time to better understand the first two tenets devoted to welcoming and valuing each student, we now disembark to observe two PSC captains in action, beginning with Stewart Morgan and his student Wesley. (*Note:* This case and all subsequent cases, as well as the names used, are fictional but based on composites of real-life students, teachers, and situations. Our intention in using a case-based approach is to extend your knowledge of the tenets and prepare you for navigating your own PSC ship.)

PSC Captain Stewart Morgan and Wesley

One way or another, we all have to find what best fosters the flowering of our humanity in this contemporary life and dedicate ourselves to it.

—Joseph Campbell

One sunny Friday, 9th grade geometry teacher Stewart Morgan sits at his desk thinking about the past week's classes. By this time, he has taught almost all 25 class sessions on his weekly schedule. Stewart typically spends much of his Friday afternoon planning period running through all his classes and thinking about each student. He has been making notes all week long about students who need a bigger challenge, students who need a gentle nudge, students he needs to confer with, students he is worried about, students he is really proud of, and students who just need a little more attention before he can establish the best next move for them. He usually ponders this list of notes over the weekend while enjoying his favorite outdoor activities.

At the top of Morgan's list is 9th grader Wesley. He has been in the same large school district since he was a 5-year-old. Wesley is biracial and the youngest of three children. His father is a dentist, and his mother works in finance.

Wesley, who is transgender, began publicly identifying as male in the summer between 8th and 9th grades. He and his parents met with school officials over the summer to change his school record to reflect his identity and to plan for his entry into high school as a male. Wesley began hormone therapy during the previous school year, resulting in significant changes to his appearance better aligned to his identity.

Wesley's parents worry he will be bullied not only by his peers but also by adults in the school. In planning with school officials over the summer, they considered how they might handle various scenarios that might come up. It is very important to Wesley and his parents that they pave the way for other transgender students to be welcomed, nurtured, and supported in the school community.

As Stewart thinks about Wesley, he notes some obvious changes in the student's demeanor over the past week. Normally, Wesley is very communicative, all smiles, outgoing, one of the first to jump right in and join Stewart in his math lesson. He easily connects with most of his classmates, especially those who aren't quite as extroverted as he is. This week, however, Wesley seemed a bit quieter than normal. A bit withdrawn. His smile was not quite as infectious and he looked down a lot, either at the objects on his desk or at the floor. Wesley was usually one of the first students in the classroom, often greeting Stewart before the teacher had a chance to say hello, and the eye contact between them was often full of unspoken but understood messages. Not this week.

Stewart wonders if Wesley might be avoiding connecting with him a bit. Anxious to know if he has done something to offend or hurt Wesley, he sends an email message to Wesley's student account requesting to meet next week for a conversation. In his response, Wesley indicates that all is well and no conversation is required, but agrees to meet Stewart at lunch on Monday anyway.

That Monday, Stewart sits at one of the student desks during his lunch period waiting when Wesley comes in.

"Wesley, it's so great to see you," he says. "Thank you for taking some of your time today to come in and see me. I've been thinking about you, and I just wanted to touch base with you for a few minutes. How was your weekend?"

"It was great," responds Wesley. "My family went to the coast, and we spent the weekend at the beach. How was yours?"

"Fantastic. My daughter's birthday was this weekend, so we had a birthday party and I built a swing set.

"Hey, listen. I'm just wondering if everything's OK. Last week, you didn't seem quite as energized as you normally do. I might be imagining things, but just wanted to check in. It just looked like you weren't as relaxed or as happy as you normally are, and I had a hard time getting you to look at me. You just seemed a bit down, a bit distracted, avoiding me. If I have done something or said something that caused you to feel this way, I want you to know I didn't do it on purpose and I have no idea what I might have done, but I want to apologize to you right now."

"Mr. Morgan, you didn't do anything. You're the one I trust the most here. I couldn't be here at school without you. I'm not mad at you or anyone else. Everything's fine, thanks."

"Then why did you just turn away and look down when you said that, Wes? Come on. I know you. You know me. You also know I'm always right here. Did something happen in my class?"

"No, sir. Nothing happened in your class."

Stewart lets the silence permeate the room. Wesley continues to look down. He is noticeably jittery, and it is obvious to Stewart that something is up.

"Wesley, can I push a bit?"

Wesley gives a barely perceptible nod, which Stewart takes as permission to proceed.

"Wesley, did something happen in another class? You said nothing happened in my class, but that seemed a bit too intentional. I know things aren't quite as smooth in other places as they are here in this room. I don't want to overreact and think that every issue or situation you'll confront is going to have something to do with your identity. What I'm trying to say is, sometimes, crap is just crap. But I hope you know, I *want* you to know, that if something happened—you just look like someone has cut a huge chunk out of your confidence, and I want to help you find it and put it back. So don't let me make more out of your demeanor than is necessary, but I also don't want to ignore something that we need to address together. And I can't read your mind, so I'm gonna stop rambling now. Are you OK?"

After what seem like hours of silence, Wesley responds.

"We got our 8th grade yearbooks last week. I hate those stupid things. I wish I had never ordered one. I just wish they had never shown up."

"You don't see yourself in that yearbook, do you? And you don't really want other people to see you in that yearbook either."

"I'm there—I just don't look like me. I look like someone else. And I'm really tired of all the stares, the glances, the stupid questions, the comments, the snide remarks. I hate it."

"I don't think any of us even thought about those yearbooks, Wesley. We made the plan this summer with you and your parents, and everything's been going well, but we didn't think of everything, did we? And we certainly forgot about these yearbooks. I'm sorry, Wesley, that the yearbook has caused you this level of grief. We overlooked this detail. Thank you for being brave enough to tell me what happened. I really appreciate it."

"I just wish people would stop asking me if I'm gay. And the sub in English was looking at the yearbook and asked me if I was new to the school. She didn't see me in the 8th grade class and asked me where I had moved here from. And then a couple of people laughed. It really sucked. I just wanted to disappear."

"Wesley, I'm sorry that happened. Listen. Lunch is about over. Can we talk again about this tomorrow? I'd like some time to think about what we—what *I*—might do to help everyone navigate this whole yearbook thing. Can we do that?"

Stewart has been studying the tenets of Powerful Student Care for some time. His own values and personality naturally gravitate toward creating a safe and nurturing space for each of his students to grow and flourish. Safeguarding Wesley's identity in his classroom space is a high priority, and he is glad to have helped lay the foundation for other students to validate, respect, and safeguard Wesley's journey. Even if others do not understand or respect the transgender journey, it is important to Stewart that they recognize Wesley's innate value as a human being. He also wants them to learn how to protect Wesley—or any individual, for that matter—from being treated poorly.

Stewart sees welcoming and valuing as foundational to the other three tenets of Powerful Student Care. Last year, he had started embedding social and emotional learning into his everyday instruction focused on helping students appreciate and respect a diversity of ideas, cultural identities, and experiences.

This year, Stewart has been working on strengthening this instruction, but also on getting students to appreciate each person's equal worth. He has been doing a lot to help students see the negative impact of stereotypes on individuals' feelings of safety and self-worth. Though he's proud of what he has accomplished so far, he knows there's a tremendous amount of work yet to be done. "One step at a time," he tells himself.

Stewart's Use of the Contemplative Practice

Stewart uses the questions from Figure 5.4 (p. 66) to develop new questions unique to Wesley (see Figure 5.5, p. 74). These questions will help Stewart better understand Wesley's experiences, how Stewart's actions have impacted those experiences, and ways to surface, interrogate, and define his mental models about Wesley's situation.

 Stewart Predicts

In talking to Wesley, Stewart realizes that not only does he have the closest connection to this student, but that Wesley views him as his lifeline at school. This human connection between teacher and student forces Stewart to think beyond just his own classroom to understand Wesley's experience throughout his entire day. Jumping a bit out of his comfort zone, Stewart decides to talk to and observe students and teachers to better understand what it means to be Wesley and to build relationships with Wesley at school. Based on his work, he identifies four areas of focus:

1. Wesley's journey is twofold: He, like his family, wants to be an example for other people. But he is also a typical 15-year-old who wants to be accepted, to have friends, to be acknowledged, to feel safe, and to thrive. While he understands intellectually

FIGURE 5.5

Stewart's Questions for Welcoming and Valuing Wesley

Welcoming and Valuing
Questions About Wesley

• Who is Wesley?
  − What are his dreams and aspirations?
  − Do I know him well enough to know what he loves?
  − What makes him sad?
  − What makes him happy?
  − What is he afraid of?
 	
• What is Wesley experiencing?
  − What did he experience at the middle school, and how is that similar to or different from what he is experiencing this year in high school?
  − How does Wesley describe his own journey?
  − What do I need to know about Wesley's specific journey to support him well?
  − How does he interact with his peers, and how do they interact with him?
  − Do students and adults understand the transgender experience based on truth, or is their understanding based on stereotypes and other misinformation?
  − What do students and adults need to learn more about to better understand the transgender identity?
  − Who can embrace Wesley's identity, and who might have difficulty doing so?
  − How do these reactions to Wesley's identity manifest themselves at school?

Questions About Me and My Actions
• What experiences at school, in my classroom, and in other classrooms extend welcoming and valuing to Wesley? • What experiences destroy or diminish Wesley's ability to feel welcomed and valued? • How have my actions safeguarded or diminished Wesley's dignity? • Given that Wesley is our only known transgender student in this school at this time, what can I do to ensure we develop our collective ability to extend welcoming and belonging to him? • How can I help ensure that the adults and students in our school embrace Wesley's identity and extend welcome given that they have very little experience interacting with someone who is transgender?
Questions to Surface, Interrogate, and Define My Mental Models
• Do I have a good enough understanding of what it means to be transgender? • How do I know that my understandings are based on truth rather than on stereotypes and other misinformation? • What more do I need to learn to better meet Wesley's needs and interests and potentially those of other students in the future?

the various reactions to his emerging identity, they can also be painful.

2. Both students and adults react to Wesley's journey in one of four ways: (1) they honor his identity and celebrate with him; (2) they are openly or quietly hostile to this new identity; (3) they just want to ignore his identity; or (4) they respond with bewilderment, asking lots of questions stemming from a lack of understanding of what it means to be transgender.

3. Stewart's actions in his own classroom have safeguarded Wesley's dignity, but by not championing this young man outside his classroom, he has allowed others to ignore Wesley, respond negatively to him, or act toward him in ways that show a lack of understanding.

4. The school put some protocols in place for transgender students, but the plan it developed with Wesley and his parents did not include opportunities for students and staff to learn, and those who helped develop the plan underestimated how much a student's identity permeates the human experience.

Having collected and analyzed as much information as he could, Stewart now moves from the Predict phase of the Contemplative Practice to the Plan For phase, where he identifies the most effective ways to address Wesley's needs and interests. In the Plan For phase, Stewart considers Wesley's needs and interest in relationship to the ways of being, knowing, and thinking foundational to Powerful Student Care.

 ## Stewart Plans

Stewart spends several days thinking about what he has discovered. He had been a part of the school team that met with Wesley and his parents last summer to plan for Wesley's first year of high school. Successfully supporting Wesley is very important both to his parents and to school staff. To the best of Stewart's knowledge, Wesley is the first transgender student at this school, though likely not the last. Stewart also recognizes that the vast majority of adults and students at the school have little understanding of gender identity, sexual orientation, and the differences between the two. Responding effectively to Wesley's needs and interests would not only be helpful to Wesley but also provide an example of how best to support other transgender students, their peers, and school staff in the future. What Stewart understands clearly is the need for Wesley (and for all students) to feel validated, respected, and supported. He understands that for each student to thrive, they must be in an environment where their dignity is upheld and their sense of self-worth is nurtured.

Using the questions in Figure 5.4 (p. 66) as a guide, Stewart ponders his next move. He does his best thinking while out on the golf course, and he knows he needs to think out loud, so he invites one of his good friends and colleagues to accompany him. In the end, Stewart realizes that Wesley's concerns about the yearbook reflect questions of identity. But it's bigger than just Wesley's emerging identity as "Wesley"; it is about the importance of identity itself: about the acceptance of one's identity and how valuing an individual for their unique worth as a human being is paramount for a student to experience feeling welcomed and valued.

To feel welcomed and valued, Wesley needs to feel that the adults and students at school see him for who he is, accept him as a human being rather than a stereotype, and value him for his uniqueness. Stewart leaves the golf course with the following questions at the forefront of his mind:

- How can I help adults and students accept someone's identity without judgment or malice?
- What is my role as a classroom teacher in helping extend the tenets of welcoming and valuing to a student beyond the confines of my classroom?
- How can we, as a school, evaluate our structures, protocols, and routines through the lens of welcoming and valuing each student?

At home that evening, as he reflects on his conversation with his colleague on the golf course, Stewart draws several conclusions:

- He has to address Wesley's experiences beyond his classroom. If he doesn't act now that he knows what's bothering Wesley, he won't be showing Wesley that he's valued. One either has a seat at the table or doesn't; one either has dignity as a human being or doesn't. Stewart knows that Wesley sees him as his lifeline and feels compelled to safeguard the boy's dignity both inside and outside his classroom.

- Students and adults need to grapple with the idea of identity and its importance to belonging and dignity.
- Students and adults need to learn how to listen to other people's stories to better understand their identities, feelings, and experiences.
- Stewart can use three of the PSC navigational instruments to help him help Wesley: values; power-sharing relationships; and structures, processes, routines, and rituals.

 ## Stewart Responds

Stewart's next step—the Respond phase of the Contemplative Practice—is to think about how he will act, how he will determine the success of his actions, and how, if at all, those actions change his mental models. Stewart's priority is to uphold and safeguard Wesley's dignity. He identifies five major responsive actions:

1. Create a series of mini-lessons and conversations for his own classroom focused on helping students see the importance of validating and accepting an individual's identity as fundamental to safeguarding dignity and nurturing belonging.
2. Engage grade-level colleagues in conversations about identity, dignity, and belonging.
3. Share his series of mini-lessons with his colleagues for potential use in their own classrooms.
4. Partner with Wesley to identify ways of talking about transgender identity and make this information available to students and adults who want to better understand the transgender experience and Wesley's own unique identity. In this partnership, Stewart will decenter himself and empower Wesley to construct learning experiences for others, leaving space for Wesley to share his lived experience and "host" other students.

5. Work with the school administration and his school team to ensure that schoolwide structures, protocols, and processes welcome and value each student and that there are accountability measures in place for when they don't.

Stewart's biggest mental model shift has to do with his own level of responsibility. Previously, Stewart was one of those teachers who focused on what he could control in his classroom. He rarely thought about what his students might experience when they weren't in his class. Now he embraces the need to rethink his role as a classroom teacher and to advocate for Wesley by informing changes at the institutional level. He now believes welcoming and valuing each student requires looking beyond the confines of just one classroom to gain a fuller understanding of what students experience.

Stewart's professional practice is steeped in self-reflection and, to some extent, critique. He recognizes that he needs to learn more about gender identity, transgender identity, sexual orientation, and the transgender journey. He also needs to learn more about Wesley's journey in particular.

Students shouldn't have their dignity as a human being upheld one hour or one class at a time. Their dignity is either safeguarded as a human birthright or it is not.

PSC Captain Meredith McNeil-Davis and Cienna

True hospitality is welcoming the stranger on her own terms.

—Henri Nouwen

Since the death of her grandmother, 8-year-old Cienna is often late to school and struggles to complete her homework. Each student in her class is expected to read to an adult for at least 20 minutes per day, and the adult is to sign off on a reading log. For every 60 minutes read, students are allowed to add a circle to the class's construction-paper "bookworm," which is proudly displayed along the walls of the classroom. Before she died, Cienna's Grandma was the one to sign Cienna's reading log and get her to school, since Veronica, Cienna's mother, had a busy work schedule. In this tight-knit family of three, Grandma had assumed primary responsibility for childcare.

Cienna is very timid and withdrawn. She avoids eye contact with adults or any of her peers. Most often she can be found playing with her stuffed animals—a menagerie gifted to her by Grandma. Cienna uses her imagination to create elaborate scenes with them.

Veronica's night shift at the local convenience store makes arriving to school on time almost impossible for Cienna. Her teacher, Meredith McNeil-Davis, is frustrated by Cienna's repeated tardiness and concerned that she's not doing her homework. She has made more than one attempt to contact Veronica, but the relationship between school and parent has become increasingly strained.

Meredith really struggles to connect with Cienna in class. It's a big class, 27 students, and she feels beleaguered because "there are so many needs." There is such a broad spectrum of achievement levels among her students that Meredith wrestles with how to respond to them all.

Monday is a particularly difficult day for Cienna. She is late again. Meredith had told the students that those with perfect attendance would have the chance to be among the "morning news" anchors on the daily news show that is televised to the entire school. Cienna's repeated tardiness disqualifies her for this opportunity. A private conversation between Meredith and Cienna on the matter does not go well: Cienna bursts into tears and hides under one of the tables in the back of the room. Meredith can't convince her to come out.

On Tuesday, Cienna reestablishes her place under the table. Meredith tries to get her to come out, but again Cienna refuses. Meredith offers her a bean bag, a rug, and another more comfortable location. Cienna declines them all. During her planning time, Meredith tries calling Veronica but gets no answer. She also puts a brief note in Cienna's backpack at the end of the day, but there is no response from Veronica on Wednesday, and the note is still in the backpack.

On Wednesday, Meredith experiences more major disruptions to her instruction than she has had in a long time. She is exhausted by it all. Meredith really wants her students to do well, but it seems as though the challenges never end, and she's particularly worn out by Cienna.

Since the debacle related to the morning news on Monday, Cienna has spent each day under the table in the corner of the room. Meredith had thought Cienna would be back to her timid self by Tuesday, sitting at her desk, but this has not been the case. When Meredith tried to get her to come out from under the table, Cienna just cried. Since she's been quiet and attentive and has even completed some of her assigned work, Meredith has allowed her to stay. But "good grief," Meredith thinks, "I can't let her stay under the table the entire week." Since there are no social workers or counselors to turn to—just other teachers, the principal, and an instructional coach who makes her really uncomfortable—she calls the principal, Mr. Dalton, and asks him to take Cienna back to his office. "Maybe he'll have better luck connecting with her than I did," Meredith thinks. Although Mr. Dalton is new to the school, Cienna likes him and goes with him without a struggle.

At the end of the day, Mr. Dalton enters Meredith's classroom as she's preparing to shut everything down and go home. Meredith expected that he would stop in sometime before she left for the day, so she isn't surprised to see him. She explains that Cienna has been under that table all week. She had reached out to her mom, but hadn't gotten any response. She didn't know her mom very well, as she had mostly dealt with Grandma. "I know this is a really tough, horrible time for Cienna after losing her grandmother," she says, "but I just couldn't look at her one more minute sitting under that table. It was making me crazy and I didn't know what else to do."

Meredith further explains that she finds Cienna to be a difficult child. "I can't get her to talk to me. When she didn't bring supplies on the first day of school, I gave her some to use, but that just upset her. She's late all the time now, so she misses our opening activities, and then she has this huge outburst because she didn't qualify to be the news anchor. I can't teach her when she's under the desk. She's not interacting with anyone, and the others aren't paying her any attention. For the rest of the students, it's as if she isn't here. But I know she's here. And I need to get her back at her desk where she belongs."

John Dalton is aware of Meredith's history of reluctance to accept assistance from others and has been increasingly concerned about her consistent refrain that she is "overwhelmed." He had been unaware of Cienna's "flight" to what must have felt like a safe space under the table until Wednesday, when Meredith asked him to intervene. He might have learned about the situation earlier in the week if he'd done his usual classroom walkthroughs, but he'd had a conference to attend on Monday and Tuesday.

The next day, John suggests to Meredith that the two of them either conduct a home visit or find a place and time that is convenient for Veronica to meet. Meredith is reluctant to leave the comfort of her classroom, but she agrees to participate if they can find a "neutral place." In truth, she is skeptical about the benefits of such a meeting, and she doubts that John will be able to arrange it since Veronica seems to be off the grid.

On Friday morning, John makes it a point to hang out around the front of the school so he can catch Veronica as she drops off Cienna. When she arrives, he successfully convinces her to go to breakfast with him and Meredith at a local café the following Monday morning at the end of her all-night shift. John arranges for a substitute teacher for the entire morning so Meredith can not only go to breakfast but also debrief and plan with him after the meeting.

On Monday at breakfast, Veronica explains that she works two part-time jobs and takes on extra shifts whenever she can. Sometimes she sees Cienna before going to work a four-hour evening shift at a local nursing home, after which she starts her shift at the convenience store. If she works an extra shift at the nursing home, she starts work at 2:00 p.m. and doesn't see Cienna until the next morning. Since her mother's death, sometimes Veronica's family members come by to care for Cienna, but most of the time Cienna has to go to their homes.

Veronica tells John and Meredith that Cienna isn't happy in school this year. At first, she says, she thought maybe Cienna's unhappiness was really about losing her grandma. But when Veronica asked Cienna why she didn't like school, she said she didn't have any friends in her class and that she thought her teacher was mad at her. She explains:

When I asked her how she had gotten that idea in her head, she told me you [looking at Meredith] were mad at her from the first day of school, when she didn't have the right box of crayons and the Kleenex and other school stuff. Recently, she told me you were also mad at her because she hasn't been reading with her aunt or her cousin, so her reading log wasn't signed. It's those little things that Mom did for her that I haven't even had a chance to think about.

Cienna had also told Veronica that she didn't like going to school on Fridays because all the other kids wore their school T-shirt that day; she didn't have one of her own because they couldn't afford it. Veronica asks John why the school doesn't just provide the shirts for every student if the goal is "school spirit or team spirit or whatever."

John asks Veronica about Cienna's dreams and aspirations, and Veronica responds that despite her shyness, "Cienna dreams of being one of the ladies on the evening news."

Meredith and John's Use of the Contemplative Practice

Using the questions from Figure 5.4 (p. 66) as a springboard, Meredith, with John's help, generates a list of questions unique to Cienna to aid her in the Predict phase of the Contemplative Practice (see Figure 5.6). Answering these questions will help Meredith better understand both Cienna's experiences and how her own actions have impacted those experiences. It will also help her look inward to surface, interrogate, and define her mental models regarding Cienna's situation.

 Meredith and John Predict

During the meeting with Veronica, Meredith heeds John's advice to "lead with her ears and not her mouth," which he also models for her throughout the conversation. John centers the conversation on Veronica's wisdom as Cienna's mom, acknowledging that it was vital for them to better support Cienna's needs and interests. Throughout the course of the conversation, five overarching ideas emerge:

FIGURE 5.6

Questions About Welcoming and Valuing Cienna

Welcoming and Valuing
Questions About Cienna

Who is Cienna?
- What are her dreams and aspirations?
- Do I know her well enough to know what she loves?
- What makes her sad?
- What makes her happy?
- What is she afraid of?

What is Cienna experiencing?
- Cienna recently lost her grandmother. Do I have good understanding of how she's working through the stages of grief?
- In what specific ways has her grandmother's death disrupted not only her life but also the stability of the family's living situation?
- How do Cienna and her mother describe her experience in my classroom?
- What do I need to know about Cienna's specific experiences to support her well?
- How is Cienna responding to me, to the principal, and to other adults?
- What is different about Cienna's relationship with me as opposed to with other adults?
- How do these differences potentially influence how she responds to me versus other adults?
- How does she interact with her peers?
- How do her peers interact with her?

Questions About Me and My Actions

- What experiences in my classroom extend welcoming and valuing to Cienna?
- What experiences in the broader school context extend welcoming and valuing to Cienna?
- What experiences destroy or diminish Cienna's ability to feel welcomed and valued in my classroom or the broader school context?
- How have I nurtured Cienna's dignity and sense of self-worth?
- How have Cienna's dignity and sense of self-worth been nurtured in the broader school context?
- What action, if any, have I or others taken to harm Cienna's dignity or sense of self-worth, and how do I know this to be the case?

Questions to Surface, Interrogate, and Define My Mental Models

- Do I have enough of an understanding of what it means to live in poverty to skillfully respond to Cienna's needs and interests?
- Do I have enough of an understanding of the complexities of trauma, grief, and loss to skillfully respond to Cienna's needs and interests?
- How do I know my understandings are based on truth rather than stereotypes and other misinformation?
- What more do I need to learn to better understand these issues and to better address Cienna's needs and interests and potentially those of other students in the future?

1. Both Veronica and Cienna are grieving their loss. They each vacillate between profound sadness and intense anger. Veronica sees herself as barely "holding on" and is worried about the impact she knows her mother's death continues to have on Cienna.

2. For both Veronica and Cienna, the loss of Grandma has been devastating not only emotionally, but materially as well, compounding their family's economic fragility.

3. Consistent in-home child care is extremely challenging because of Veronica's working hours.

4. School adds to Cienna's trauma. Veronica told John and Meredith that Cienna isn't happy in school this year.

5. Meredith knows very little about Cienna. As a result of the conversation with Veronica, she now better understands Cienna's tardiness and inconsistency with homework. She reflects on Cienna's reaction to being the only student without school supplies on the first day of school and the fact that the supplies must be hard for them to afford. She also understands the additional stress the school has inadvertently imposed on Cienna and her mother with the expectation of buying the school T-shirt.

Having collected and analyzed as much information as she could, Meredith, with John's help, now moves from the Predict phase of the Contemplative Practice to the Plan For phase, where she identifies the most effective ways to address Cienna's needs and interests. In this phase, Meredith and John consider Cienna's needs and interests in relation to the ways of being, knowing, and thinking foundational to Powerful Student Care.

 ## Meredith and John Plan

John and Meredith meet in John's office after the meeting with Veronica, which had lasted about 90 minutes, to discuss the overarching ideas that emerged. John begins the conversation by telling Meredith he feels responsible for some of the marginalizing experiences that have contributed to Cienna's distress. He explains that he had not wanted to be heavy-handed about changing things in his first year and didn't want to change the way things were done until he had had a chance to earn people's trust.

John wasn't comfortable with how the school had handled the school T-shirts. If the T-shirts were meant to symbolize welcoming and belonging, what message were they sending to the students who didn't have the means to purchase them? John tells Meredith that he should have shared his concerns with staff and worked with them to determine a more equitable process. He believes staff needs to be open-minded and humble enough to consider how some of their policies, routines, and rituals may unintentionally disregard the needs and interests of some students.

Meredith hadn't really thought about the T-shirts in that way. For as long as she could remember, the school had always expected students to purchase them. She wonders what her colleagues would think if this schoolwide tradition were to change. She isn't even sure what she herself thinks. She is also surprised that John begins their meeting by talking about what he could have done differently, since she had anticipated that she would be in the hot seat.

Following the discussion with Veronica, Meredith realizes she doesn't know much about a lot of her students. When John asks her, "How do you try to build relationships with your students?" Meredith's first thought is, "When do I even have time to build relationships?" Instead, she says, "Well, I guess I just try to get to know them little by little throughout the year, informally. It's not like I do explicit activities to build relationships. I don't mean to sound defensive, but when would I have time to do relationship-building activities?"

Even as she says this, Meredith thinks back to how much more intentional she had been in building relationships with students during her first years of teaching. That was before she had her own children and before the pressure to raise test scores eclipsed everything else.

"What do you want your students to experience in your classroom? What do you want them to feel?" John asks.

"I want them to feel safe and happy," says Meredith, "and when I think about Cienna, I know she doesn't feel either of those things very much these days."

John and Meredith continue to talk. They discuss the book study the staff was just completing related to trauma-sensitive learning environments and what it might teach them about helping Cienna. They also discuss the school's SEL program and the five core SEL competencies. John emphasizes one competency in particular: developing students' self-awareness. He discusses the importance of helping students better understand who they are and affirming their developing identities. He again notes that school policies and procedures related to school supplies and T-shirts have likely had an adverse impact on Cienna's sense of belonging, dignity, and self-worth.

Meredith acknowledges that Cienna was disappointed when she wasn't able to add to the bookworm because even though she brought in her reading log faithfully, it often hadn't been signed. Feeling somewhere between defensive and guilty, Meredith says to John, "Cienna hasn't been able to add to the bookworm, and that's a really big thing to the kids. I'll admit, I had no idea Cienna's dream was to anchor the nightly news. No wonder she was so upset when she didn't get a turn to broadcast the morning announcements."

Meredith and John discuss the importance of building relationships with students, and especially of supporting each student to feel welcomed and valued. Meredith reluctantly says, "John, I feel like there is no time for building a sense of community or for really getting to know the students. How do I fit it all in?" John responds unequivocally: "Meredith, there is no more important use of your time, and I am here to support you in rethinking how you are currently doing things."

John shares with Meredith some materials from the PSC workshops he recently attended. He asks her to review what it means to unconditionally welcome and value each student and promises to share what else he has learned about developing a sense of community in classrooms. Meredith and John resolve to meet again to develop a plan for integrating the two tenets of welcoming and valuing into Meredith's everyday practices and identify navigational instruments she can use with her entire class and with Cienna specifically. Before the next meeting, Meredith agrees to spend some time with Cienna to get to know her better and to begin gaining her trust.

Meredith and John's next step is to think about the logistics of the actions Meredith will take, how to determine the success of her actions, and how their mental models will change as a result (if they change at all).

 ## Meredith and John Respond

Meredith begins to integrate various curricular activities and employ instructional methods intended to develop students' self-awareness and identities (e.g., identity mapping, I Am From poems); connect students to each other (e.g., cooperative learning, academic discourse, morning meetings); and co-create a sense of community through collective and individual contributions (e.g., meaningful roles and jobs, co-designed norms or rules, developmentally appropriate antibias and antiracist work).

Meredith integrates into her daily routines a few basic strategies for connecting with individual students or small groups to get to know them better and to allow them to know her (e.g., rotating two-minute conversations with individual students, rotating weekly brown-bag lunches with small groups of students, conducting student surveys).

Knowing that Cienna has a flight-or-freeze response to stress, Meredith works with her to help identify when her "downstairs brain" (Siegal, 2003; cited in Souers & Hall, 2016) is in charge and shares strategies she can use to move to her "upstairs" brain.

Meredith recognizes that her past practice had failed to uphold Cienna's human dignity. She is willing to now decenter herself, working with Cienna to find ways for her to complete her homework at school on days when she doesn't bring in a signed reading log. In this way, Cienna can contribute to the bookworm with her peers. Meredith also develops a more equitable way to select students for the school's televised morning news.

It's Your Turn!

Identify one student who you believe is not adequately welcomed, valued, or both.

1. What is the student's name?

2. Are you worried the student is not being welcomed, valued, or both?

3. What questions will you ask yourself to interpret all available information?

4. How will you use this information to pinpoint the most effective way to address this student's interests and needs?

5. How does your plan incorporate an ethic of hospitality, cultural humility, equity through belonging and dignity, and other areas of your expertise as well as the navigational instruments for building community?

6. How will you put your thinking into responsive action?

6

Each Student Is Here to Do Well, Develop Self-Efficacy, Cultivate Agency, and Experience Joy in Learning

There is no power for change greater than a community discovering what it cares about.

—Dr. Margaret Wheatley

Our intention in making stops at each of the next three ports of call on our way to The Harbor (see Figure 6.1, p. 90) is to deepen your understanding of the last three tenets of community: *each student is here to do well; each student is here to develop self-efficacy and agency;* and *each student is here to experience the joy of learning academically, socially, and emotionally.*

In Chapter 5, we defined what it means to welcome and value each student and identified some barriers to extending these two tenets of Powerful Student Care to each student. In this chapter, we define the remaining three tenets and explicate what we intend for students to experience when we trust students' innate intention to do well, develop student self-efficacy and agency, and facilitate joy-filled learning experiences.

FIGURE 6.1

The Map to The Harbor: The Last Three Ports of Call

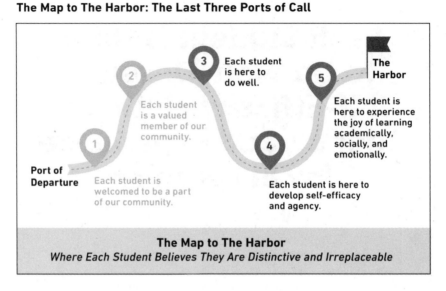

The Map to The Harbor
Where Each Student Believes They Are Distinctive and Irreplaceable

What Does It Mean to Believe Students "Want" to Do Well?

As I (Kathleen) thought about this tenet and what it means, I was reminded of the many teachers I have met in high-poverty schools across the United States who believe in their students' intentions and their potential. These teachers hold high expectations for each student. One teacher, especially, came to mind—a high school mathematics teacher I will call Andi Hopp. At the time I met Andi, her state had recently implemented a requirement for all graduating students to pass an end-of-course exam in Algebra II. Most students passed the exam in either 10th or 11th grade.

In my conversation with Andi, I discovered that she had agreed to help students who had not passed the exam to do so in the upcoming school year. In the end, all but two students passed. She told me this was only a partial success because she had "lost" two students who had dropped out of school. The system had failed to respond to these students' needs for years.

When I asked Andi what she thought had contributed to the success of the students who had passed the exam, she relayed stories of her efforts to build students' foundational skills by employing strategies she had used as an elementary teacher. She also described building a sense of community and camaraderie among the students so they would support each other.

"The kids began calling themselves Hopp's Highflyers," she said. "At first they were just being sarcastic, but as they began to feel more confident, I think they sort of took pride in that name." She told us about worrying that some students would not be ready to pass the exam even though they had grown a great deal:

> Actually, I was afraid for myself, because I told the kids I believed in them, but sometimes there was a kernel of doubt that would creep into my mind. I just wasn't sure *we* were going to pull it off. I really believed the kids could learn what they needed to learn, and I told them so. In fact, one day I told one of the kids, "I am going to believe in you until you believe in yourself." That kid, by the way, had begun class that day telling me he was "done with this sh**!"

Andi embodies the third tenet of Powerful Student Care—each student is here to do well—and her belief in her students was undoubtedly a game-changer for them.

What the Research Says

In his book *Motivation and Personality*, Abraham Maslow (1954) coined the term *positive psychology* to describe a branch of humanistic psychology focused less on dysfunction and damage in humans and more on their virtues and potential. As Zacarian and colleagues (2017) put it,

> Positive psychology is a belief that, as humans, we all want to be the best that we can be and it is in our nature to strive toward what Maslow refers to as our self-actualized potential. It positions human

behavior as being driven by the desire to lead richly meaningful and fulfilling lives. (p. 15)

Thirty years later, Edward Deci and Richard Ryan (1985), themselves pioneers in the field of positive psychology, drew from Maslow's concepts to introduce self-determination theory. This theory holds that self-determination is the "ability of humans to make choices and manage their lives, which plays an important role in our psychological health and well-being" (Cherry, 2021, para. 1) and that humans are "driven by the need to grow and gain fulfillment" (para. 5). Self-determination theory focuses primarily on intrinsic motivation and suggests that human beings are actively oriented toward growth. As we open ourselves to new experiences and tackle novel challenges (which is how we learn), the theory posits, we develop an integrated sense of self (paras. 6–7).

Believing in our students' innate intention to do well isn't just something we *should* do; it is something we *must* do. It is critically important for supporting each student's infinite potential. More than four decades of research shows unequivocally that teachers' beliefs and assumptions about students' potential to learn matters a great deal (Brophy, 1982; Good & Nichols, 2001; Gregory & Huang, 2013; Jussim & Harber, 2005; Rist, 1970/2000; Rubie-Davies, 2015; Rubie-Davies et al., 2006; Weinstein, 2002).

Teachers' expectations—high or low, negative or positive—influence students' learning, and this influence can be particularly strong for students from stigmatized groups (McKown & Weinstein, 2002; Nichols & Good, 2004). Internalization of low teacher expectations can become a self-fulfilling prophecy resulting in a sustained pattern of low achievement. Teachers tend to hold lower or negative expectations for students from stigmatized and marginalized groups (Beady & Hansell, 1981; Nichols & Good, 2004; Rubie-Davies et al., 2006; Solomon et al., 1996). This is unfortunate, as high expectations can provide a "protective factor" in the lives of those same students that supports their learning (Gregory & Huang, 2013).

The brain's neuroplasticity offers another rationale for believing in our students' positive intentions. Advancements in neuroscience demonstrate that our brain can "rewire itself" to "overcome the odds stacked against us… giving us an enormous amount of hope" for working with all students but particularly those living with "trauma, violence, and chronic stress" (Zacarian et al., 2017, p. 17).

Each child's innate human desire to self-actualize is supported by the view that intelligence is *growable*. Carol Dweck (2006) defines a growth mindset as the belief that all students can succeed when we teach them to do the following:

- Believe in their ability to take on the challenge and complexity of learning
- Value and develop the habit of persistence
- Understand the importance of expending effort
- Inspire them to do more than they thought they could

Demonstrating our belief in students must go beyond telling them we believe in them or telling ourselves and others that we have high expectations for all our students. As Richard Curwin (2012) points out, "kids have built-in crap detectors"—a term he borrows from Postman and Weingartner (1971), authors of *Teaching as a Subversive Activity*. "These words matter only if they are true and if you demonstrate them by your actions.… [Students] can tell if you don't mean it" (2012, para. 7).

What Do We Intend Students to Experience When We Trust in Their Intentions?

At this point, take a minute or two to study the information in Figure 6.2 (p. 94). In demonstrating to students our belief that they come to school to do well, we affirm their innate desire for self-determination. According to Deci and Ryan (2017), becoming self-determined learners fulfills students' need for connection, autonomy, and competency.

Cultivating Optimistic Learners

Educators play a critical role in the development of students' mental models of themselves as learners. They support students in developing optimism by creating the conditions in which their strengths and assets are made evident to and are mirrored for them. Grove and Glasser (2007) describe this process as helping students acknowledge and build their *inner wealth*. All people are driven by an innate need for self-actualization and self-determination, even when their behavior or achievement suggest otherwise.

FIGURE 6.2

Defining What It Means to Trust in Students' Innate Intention to Do Well

The Tenet	What It Means	What We Say Directly to Students	What We Want Students to Say Directly to Us
Each student is here to do well.	**If** we absolutely affirm each student's innate human intention to do well and embrace each student's need to grow, make choices, and connect with others... **Then** each student develops an image of themselves as a capable learner cognizant of their strengths and assets and free from the harm of stereotypes and implicit bias.	"We know you come here every day wanting to do well."	"I am here because I want to do well, and I know you will help me do well. I am trusted. I am capable. I am supported."

Educators must be keen observers of their students, providing feedback related to what students do and don't do with the strengths they bring with them (and those they are developing), which may not be evident to the students themselves. This may require us to break down complex tasks or routines to identify students' strengths. It may also require us to surface and rethink our assumptions about each student's motivation or behavior so we can "see" the strength the student is demonstrating. Glasser (2011) refers to this process as creating "miracles from molecules" (cited in Zacarian et al., 2017, p. 43).

Recall the story of Meredith and Cienna in Chapter 5. Even though her reading log was often unsigned, Cienna returned it to school each day and explained that she was not able to read with an adult the night before. Had Meredith been attuned to making "miracles out of molecules," she might have congratulated Cienna on the personal responsibility she was exhibiting by bringing the log back. She may also have discovered that Cienna was motivated to complete her reading assignment and acknowledge this motivation as an asset.

For students who are stigmatized and marginalized, cultivating optimism will require educators to recognize the legacy of damage caused by stereotypes and the role implicit bias plays in their schooling. As we previously mentioned, Alexs Pate (2020) calls for educators to develop classroom learning environments in which students experience innocence. He explains: "You may think that the innocence of a child is self-evident. Yet, in some strange but undeniable way, our culture robs children of color and most other marginalized children of a reasonable chance to know and experience what I am calling innocence" (pp. 2–3).

Students who experience guilt by association due to stereotypes can find it hard to develop an optimistic view of themselves as learners (Aronson, 2004; Steele, 2010). Innocent classrooms are created when we come to know our students deeply enough to identify their "good," says Pate (2020, p. 37). Drawing from Aristotle, Pate defines a student's "good" as "that for the sake of which all else is done" (p. 37). In other words, a student's "good" is that which motivates them.

Take a moment to dwell on what we are claiming here. At base, all humans are driven by the need for growth and fulfillment (Deci & Ryan, 1985; Maslow, 1954), and educators are vital in helping them to "live out" that basic motivation. We help students develop a mental model of themselves as learners that includes optimism. This entails assisting them in identifying their strengths and creating a learning environment where they are freed from the negative narratives they experience outside the classroom. It also necessitates building students' confidence and upholding their self-worth by assuring them that we are on their team.

Being on the Same Team

Through the provision of Powerful Student Care, educators build students' self-confidence and uphold their self-worth with the aim of nurturing self-determination in two ways: by promoting a sense that learning is an endeavor "we are all in together"—developing a sense of community (our way of being), extending unconditional welcome to each member of the community (Tenet 1), and valuing each member's identity (Tenet 2)—and by assuming the perspective that we are on the same team with our students (Tenet 3).

Martin Haberman (1995) coined the term *Star Teacher* to describe effective teachers who enact 15 "functions" that he identified in his research. Valerie Hill-Jackson and colleagues (2019) later distilled Haberman's 15 functions to 7 dispositions. One of the dispositions relates to Star Teachers' mental model for supporting their most vulnerable students and reflects a perspective that Haberman (1995) sums up as "You [the student] and Me [the teacher] Against the Material" (p. 85). He explains that Star Teachers "establish a form of rapport with children that clearly communicates the teacher and children are on the same side." He provides an example of what a teacher who assumes this disposition might say to a student:

> It is us, we together, joined in a common effort, against the material, which can sometimes be tricky or difficult or more complicated than it seems. But we can do it together and both derive a sense of joy and well-being: you—the student—because of the thrill that comes from learning and me—the teacher—because I've helped create a situation that will enable you to succeed. (p. 86)

When you're on the same team as your students, coaching and facilitating becomes the primary model for teaching. "Coaches do not merely serve as sources of knowledge," Haberman notes. "They show how, they interest, they involve, and they seek ways to connect subjects with the children's backgrounds and experiences" (p. 86).

We demonstrate our belief in students' intent to do well by cultivating optimism, which positively affects students' mental models of themselves as learners. When they know we're on their team, they see their greatness and inherent value in our reflections of them (Pate, 2020; Zacarian et al., 2017), and they begin to develop self-efficacy and agency.

What Do We Mean by Self-Efficacy and Agency?

Self-efficacy is confidence in one's abilities (Chuter, 2020). Drawing from Bandura's (2006) conceptualization of self-efficacy, Jillianne Code (2020) further defines it as "a functional self-awareness in which students reflect on their personal efficacy, thoughts, actions, the meaning of their pursuits, and make corrective adjustments if necessary" to reach their goals (p. 2). According to Margolis and McCabe (2006), self-efficacy manifests from four sources:

- *Enactive mastery*—Generally, teachers can capitalize on the natural tendency of struggling learners to evaluate task-performance information by giving them tasks of moderate challenge, that is, tasks they can succeed on with moderate effort....
- *Vicarious experience*—Teachers can take advantage of this source of self-efficacy by regularly and systematically having struggling learners observe models perform targeted skills or learning strategies, live or on video....
- *Verbal persuasion*—By regularly stating that learners will succeed on specific tasks, tasks on which they do succeed, and following up with task-specific feedback outlining what learners did that produced success, teachers can capitalize on this important source of self-efficacy....
- *Physiological reaction*—To use struggling learners' physiological reactions or states to strengthen self-efficacy, teachers or counselors might teach them relaxation techniques and ways to challenge irrational thoughts that provoke exaggerated or inaccurate physiological responses. (p. 219)

Self-efficacy is a necessary competency for the development of agency, which is "the power to originate action" (Bandura, 2001, p. 3; cited in Code, 2020). "It is present in the ability of people to regulate and control their cognition, motivation, and behavior through the influence of existing self-beliefs (i.e., self-efficacy)" (Code, 2020, p. 2). *Agentic* is the term used to describe people who have a sense of agency. Such people are able to exert influence that alters their social and cultural contexts.

In the context of education, developing students' agency means increasing their capability in three areas: self-efficacy, self-awareness, and self-regulation. Given the U.S. policy emphasis on social-emotional learning (SEL) in the past decade, these concepts are likely familiar to most educators. The Collaborative for Academic, Social, and Emotional Learning (CASEL) (n.d.), a leading organization in the field of SEL, suggests students should develop competency in five areas, two of which are self-awareness and self-regulation/management (the other three are social awareness, relationship skills, and responsible decision making).

Agentic students are optimistic about their ability (self-efficacy) to tackle challenging tasks, and each time they successfully do so, their self-efficacy is strengthened. Their understanding of their personal values and priorities (self-awareness) shapes their approach to learning (e.g., goal setting, planning, purpose finding, and decision making), and they are able to direct their effort toward specific long- and short-term goals (self-regulation), monitor their progress, manage their time, and use effective learning strategies (Chuter, 2020).

To consider student agency in the context of Powerful Student Care, we first return to our philosophical roots. An ethic of hospitality reminds educators that

> the spaces of education are not *their* spaces, spaces they own or should consider under their control, but rather spaces into which they have been received and whose purpose is to give place to students. For teachers who work in neighborhoods where they do not live, this is an especially important reminder…. This ethic, at every turn, poses the question, "Will you let the other take place?" (Ruitenberg, 2011, pp. 33–35)

We cannot foster agency in our students unless we are willing to share power in the "spaces of education" with them—the physical, curricular, instructional, and relational spaces. This requires us to decenter ourselves so that students can develop self-awareness and practice self-regulation. Recall Stewart, the teacher in Chapter 5 who decentered himself to share a "space of education" with Wesley. In this shared space, Wesley enhanced his self-awareness as he co-created lessons for other students related to transgender identity.

Students need choice and opportunities to self-direct their learning. Giving them voice must be a priority. Students who feel they have a voice are seven times more likely to be academically motivated than students who don't (Quaglia Institute, 2016). We need to form learning partnerships with students where we listen to them and incorporate their feedback into teaching and learning, community building, and care and management of the physical space.

Learning partnerships are crucial for building students' self-efficacy and congruent with the theoretical foundation for Powerful Student Care. The practice of cultural humility compels us to form such partnerships *because there are two people with expertise about learning and the learner in the room—the teacher and the student.* "By approaching learning partnerships with humility, educators… value [students'] stories, dreams, and aspiration with attention to relevance" (Tinkler & Tinkler, 2016, p. 199). Such learning partnerships are the means by which we guide students' "mastery experiences" and provide them with "verbal persuasion" (e.g., providing timely and accurate feedback; identifying strengths and assets; connecting learning with cultural funds of knowledge, aspirations, and interests). Before continuing, take a moment to study the information in Figure 6.3 (p. 100).

What Do We Intend Students to Feel and Experience When They Are Self-Efficacious and Agentic?

Students with agency tend to do better academically than those who lack it. They actively seek assistance and clarification from their teachers and are willing to engage in activities that challenge them and require them to take risks. They are willing to learn from their mistakes and seek ways to personally relate to their learning as well as pursue means for growth and improvement. They are more likely to participate in extracurricular activities, assume leadership roles, and take action related to social issues that matter to them. They are comfortable sharing their voice and will advocate for change "rather than turning a blind eye or feeling disempowered to act" (Chuter, 2020, para. 13). Agentic students are more likely to become adults who have a secure sense of self-worth, are more likely to enter into healthy personal relationships, and are better prepared for citizenship in a democracy.

Powerful Student Care supports the development of agency by ensuring a learning environment where students can increasingly become self-determined human beings—where they can fulfill their desire for connection, competence, and autonomy, all of which are instrumental to the development of agency. We do this by unconditionally welcoming them into our community and valuing who they are and who they are becoming.

FIGURE 6.3

Defining What It Means to Trust in Students to Develop Self-Efficacy and Agency

The Tenet	What It Means	What We Say Directly to Students	What We Want Students to Say Directly to Us
Each student is here to develop self-efficacy and agency.	**If** we unqualifiedly and capably foster each student's belief in their ability to thrive and their capability to do what is needed to flourish and we embrace each student's need to share the learning space with us… **Then** each student will experience self-efficacy and agency as they feel confident and optimistic about their potential to succeed; gain understanding of themselves as a capable learner; and purposefully engage in the learning process as co-creator of the physical, curricular, instructional, and relational space.	"We want each of you to believe in your own ability to thrive as much as we do."	"I can do this. I am confident. I have power."

What Do We Mean by the Joy of Learning?

In 1938, John Dewey asked the question "What avail is it to win pre-scribed amounts of information about geography and history, to win the ability to read or write, if in the process the individual loses his soul?" (p. 49).

In 1970, Paulo Freire argued that education is

an act of depositing, in which the students are the depositories and the teacher is the depositor. Instead of communicating, the teacher issues communiques and makes deposits which the students patiently receive, memorize, and repeat. This is the "banking" con-cept of education, in which the scope of action allowed to the stu-dents extends only as far as receiving, filing, and storing the deposits. They do, it is true, have the opportunity to become collectors or cataloguers of the things they store. But in the last analysis, it is the people themselves who are filed away through the lack of creativity, transformation and knowledge in this (at best) misguided system. (p. 72)

In 1984, after conducting a landmark study of U.S. schooling, John Goodlad concluded that "boredom is a disease of epidemic pro-portions" and posed a simple but compelling question: "Why are our schools not places of joy?" (p. 242).

In 2009, Kirsten Olson documented 11 ways in which contem-porary schooling wounds people. At the top of her list are "everyday losses of pleasure in learning."

In 2012, Alice Udvari-Solner asserted that schools around the world "instill anxiety, boredom, and impede students' innate interest and spirit to learn. The implicit messages sent to students and fami-lies are that schooling is simply work and drudgery, if you are having a sense of enjoyment or fun, learning will not be effective, and the joy should be earned or even reserved for environments other than school" (p. 1666).

Too few classroom learning experiences tap into our innate human desire for joy. Udvari-Solner (2012) defines *joyful learning* as "the positive intellectual and emotional state of learner(s) ... [a] state or experience [that] is achieved when an individual or group is deriving pleasure and a sense of satisfaction from the process of learning" (p. 1665). The joy of learning can be passive or active. When joy is passive, students experience pleasure based on features they did not have a hand in creating, such as soft lighting or background music. When joy is active, it is the result of student initiative, such as persisting on a challenging task. The joy of learning can be cognitive and slowly progressive (such as when persisting on a challenging task), or it can be physiological and quick (such as a sudden reaction to a new discovery or experiment (Varila & Viholainen, 2000; cited in Rantala & Maatta, 2012).

Joyful learning is "one of the transcendent experiences of human life, one that offers meaning and a sense of connection in ways that few other activities can" (Olson, 2009, pp. 30–31). Extending the tenet of joyful learning to students means fundamentally altering existing connections between students and their purposes for learning, interactions between and among students, and connections between teacher and student. "The live connection between two human beings in the instructional environment—the emotional experience of this interaction—is the soul of educative practice" (p. 166).

The joy of learning occurs both spontaneously and by design in classrooms, with teachers being critical to the shaping of students' affective experience in school (Cronqvist, 2021; Olson, 2009; Rantala & Maatta, 2012). Before you continue reading, take a moment to reflect on the information in Figure 6.4.

What Do We Intend Students to Experience When Learning Is Joyful?

Think about the last time you learned something well. How would you describe the experience? What did you feel? What motivated you to learn this particular thing? Was curiosity a factor? What role did others play in your learning? What contributed to your successes? How did you view risk taking and failure? What role did discovery or inquiry play? Did you have the opportunity to make choices? At what point did you feel competent? Did you experience joy along the way? In what context did your learning occur?

FIGURE 6.4

**Defining What It Means to Trust in Students
to Experience the Joy of Learning**

The Tenet	What It Means	What We Say Directly to Students	What We Want Students to Say Directly to Us
Each student is here to experience the joy of learning academically, socially, and emotionally.	**If** we unreservedly nurture each student's innate human desire to learn and embrace their need for appropriate stimulation, challenge, creativity, support, and choice… **Then** each student will find their purpose for learning, make authentic meaning from their learning, and connect to other human beings through their learning, all of which together will be experienced as a profound feeling of academic, social, and emotional joy.	"We want you to think that what you are learning is interesting, that it challenges you in just the right way, and that it is relevant to your life."	"This is the place where I learn and grow. This is the place that stretches me. I am motivated here. I am excited here. I am curious here. I feel wonder. I find purpose here."

"Many of our greatest joys in life are related to our learning," writes Steve Wolk (2008). "Unfortunately, most of that joyful learning takes place outside of school" (p. 10). Teachers can facilitate conditions that affirm and support students' innate motivation to find joy in learning and must do what they can not to drive away this motivation in the classroom (Rantala & Maatta, 2012).

Experiencing the joy of learning enhances humans' cognitive, social, and emotional capacities:

- Neurochemical research and neuroimaging show that cognition and information processing are improved when people have enjoyable experiences engaging in learning activities that are relevant to them.
- When people engage in novel, stimulating, and appropriately challenging learning activities, the reticular activating

system (RAS) is stimulated, leading to improved attention and alertness.

- Dopamine is released when learning is pleasurable, which also stimulates our attention and memory centers.
- The limbic system appears to attach emotional significance to information, which improves cognition and associates positive memories with the learning when people experience low levels of stress, feel safe and trusted, and are engaged and motivated. (Udvari-Solner, 2012; Willis, 2007)

Research on the concept of joyful learning is limited, particularly in the United States (Udvari-Solner, 2012). This fact is not surprising, but it should concern us. Education policy is silent on the issue of joy, and practice reflects policy. Nonetheless, research in other countries such as Finland and Sweden (e.g., Cronqvist, 2021; Rantala & Maatta, 2012) can be informative.

Rantala and Maatta (2012) observe that the *"elements* of emotional experience are similar all over the world, but emotional experiences are not" (p. 89). In other words, context matters:

> The joy of learning appears differently in every teacher's classroom. There are many ways to establish a learning environment that enables students to experience the joy of learning.... Teacher-hood involves more than teaching... it is a way of being a human being.... The most important thing is for every teacher to consider the joy of learning or lack of it in his/her classroom and to think of ways to provide his/her [students] an opportunity to experience joy. (p. 101)

The joy of learning is a multidimensional construct (Rantala & Maatta, 2012) with considerable benefits:

- When students experience success and the satisfaction of task completion, their self-efficacy is fortified, motivation is enhanced, and capacity to solve problems is increased.
- When students are allowed an appropriate level of autonomy (choice, freedom, decision-making authority), they are able to pursue their curiosity, use their creativity, and engage their imagination.

- When students engage in "a productive struggle" and success-fully tackle challenging but manageable tasks where the goal is clear, they strengthen their self-confidence, enhance their self-respect, deepen their courage to take risks, and are more likely to experience the positive psychological state of flow (Csikszentmihalyi, 1990).
- When students' learning is personalized, their innate desire to grow and strive for well-being is reinforced, they "own" their learning, and they may engage for longer periods of time.
- When students work with peers and interested, invested teachers, the joy of learning becomes integrated into relation-ships and students' cognitive, social, and emotional skills are enhanced.
- When students are afforded a voice in their own learning and authority to make decisions, they develop agency for learning, are more engaged in the learning process, and make more aca-demic progress.
- When learning is relevant to students, their innate desire to grow and strive for well-being is reinforced, their identity is affirmed, and their interests and aspirations are honored.
- When students' dignity is upheld, they are not self-conscious and limited by anxiety or doubt in their ability to learn, allow-ing them to focus on learning tasks.
- When students are provided time for breaks from formalized intellectual and emotional engagement, their brains can recu-perate from the stresses of learning and students can interact with peers in ways that synergistically support the joy of learn-ing in the classroom.

Teachers are the main facilitators of joy in learning. They can pro-vide opportunity for joy or be an obstacle to it. Teachers who facilitate the joy of learning commit to creating interest; being encouraging; providing variety in learning activities; offering room for challenge, creativity, and choice; and being supportive and fair to all students (Cronqvist, 2021). Put simply, teachers need to be keen kid-watchers, expert question-askers, and dedicated relationship-builders. (See

Appendix B on p. 159 for experiences that promote the joy of learning, actions educators take to promote it, and necessary learning conditions.)

According to Udvari-Solner (2012), "joyful learning challenges habitual or traditional teaching paradigms and emphasizes the creation of positive and even enjoyable learning processes" (p. 1666). Prioritizing the joy of learning requires that we reimagine more noble purposes for schooling and transform the reasons and ways we approach exchanges with learners. Schooling must no longer be "primarily about creating workers and test takers, but rather about nurturing human beings" (Wolk, 2008, p. 10).

Barriers to Affirming Students' Innate Intentions, Developing Students' Self-Efficacy and Agency, and Facilitating Joy-Filled Learning

There are four main obstacles to the three tenets discussed in this chapter: a fixed mindset, transactional teaching and learning, deficit thinking, and implicit bias.

Fixed Mindset

After studying thousands of children, Stanford University researcher Carol Dweck (2006) developed a theory about learning and intelligence. She uses the terms *fixed mindset* and *growth mindset* to represent two ends of a continuum of beliefs related to intelligence. People with a fixed mindset believe intelligence is static and cannot be developed, whereas those with a growth mindset believe intelligence can be improved and increased with learning and practice.

Decades of scholarship show a limited consensus as to what constitutes intelligence (Goldstein et al., 2015). As Arthur Jensen (1972) points out, intelligence depends on how we measure it, so it is fundamentally not fixed. Studies revealing that IQ scores can change with intervention (Goldstein et al., 2015) and emerging research on the neuroplasticity of the brain (Zacarian et al., 2017) both suggest a refutation of the construct that intelligence is a fixed human attribute.

Belief in the infinite human potential of each student is a bedrock principle of Powerful Student Care. Research shows that measures of intelligence are subject to bias and misuse that can cause harm, particularly to people of color and other marginalized populations (Muhammad, 2020; Steele, 2010). Gholdy Muhammad (2020) notes that the development of students' intellect is "connected to happiness, which is the hope of our children and an inalienable right" (p. 108). We can affirm students' innate desire to learn and grow, support them in the development of self-efficacy and agency, and ensure that their learning is joy-filled only when we believe each student's intellect can be developed.

Transactional Teaching and Learning

Viewing teaching and learning as transactional rather than relational is not compatible with Powerful Student Care. A transactional perspective sees education as an exchange: "I teach, you learn. If you don't learn, I may give you a few more chances, but if you *still* don't learn, then there is probably something wrong with you." Unfortunately, blaming the student is all too commonplace in schools.

Drawing on the work of Donna Hicks (2011), Cobb and Krownapple (2019) tell us that "all human clashes are the result of feeling a threat to or loss of some aspect of our dignity.... Humans are instinctively (although not always consciously) aware of the extreme vulnerability of human dignity" (p. 126). When students fail to learn what the teacher has attempted to teach, the teacher too often resorts to blaming the student as a way of saving face. Blaming and saving face are two ways in which people are tempted to violate another's dignity.

Deficit Thinking

Deficit thinking is the "notion that students (particularly low-income, minority students) fail in school because they have inherent inadequacies that obstruct the learning process (e.g., limited intelligence, lack of motivation, and inadequate home socialization)" (Valencia, 2010). It reinforces the idea that there is a universal norm (usually white and middle-class) against which all those who are not part of this normative group are compared. Deficit thinking is operating when we blame students, parents, cultures, or communities for poor student outcomes.

Cobb and Krownapple (2019) note that, in the wake of No Child Left Behind (2002) legislation, there was increased demand for professional development focused on "fixing" perceived deficiencies among certain groups of students, their families, and their cultural beliefs and traditions. "Perhaps well-intentioned, the assumptions behind this demand were that quick fixes could boost the performance of historically underserved groups," they write. "However, this thinking reduces students to a single aspect of their identity or demography, thus dismissing their dignity and humanity" (pp. 128–129).

When educators act from a deficit perspective, we do not accept responsibility for student learning, which entails interrogating our mental models and going back to the drawing board when students struggle to learn what has been taught (Budge & Parrett, 2018). We also fail to consider the many systemic factors that influence and constrain students' achievement, and we miss the opportunity to capitalize on the strengths, assets, and funds of knowledge students bring to school.

The National Academies of Sciences, Engineering, and Medicine (2018) stress the importance of shifting from a deficit model "to a view that each student brings a unique combination of assets to the classroom and every student's learning is fostered in an environment that takes those assets into account. A key dimension of creating equitable classrooms involves building a classroom environment where all students' ideas are valued" (p. 141). As Zacarian and colleagues (2017) put it,

> Our thinking needs to shift from what we believe is not happening and is impossible to what is happening and possible. To do this we must take time to
>
> - Identify students' existing strengths.
> - Honor, value, and acknowledge these strengths.
> - Help students become aware of their strengths.
> - Build instructional programming that boosts social ties and networks by drawing from students' strengths. (p. 14)

Clearly, deficit thinking poses a significant barrier to the provision of Powerful Student Care. We cannot trust in our students' intent to do well, nurture their self-efficacy and sense of agency, or provide the autonomy needed to experience the joy of learning if we view our students through a deficit lens.

Implicit Bias

We all harbor unconscious biases related to such issues as race, gender, socioeconomic status, religion, geography, and sexual orientation. "These biases influence us even when they are in direct opposition to our espoused beliefs—and sometimes in opposition to our own lived experience," writes Sarah Fiarman (2016). "That is because unconscious biases are just that—*unconscious*. We aren't aware of them and how they influence our behavior" (p. 10).

Educators make hundreds of decisions daily that are potentially based on unconscious biases. Studies show that even when academic achievement is the same, teachers tend to have lower expectations for their students of color and who live in poverty than for others (Beady & Hansell, 1981; Nichols & Good, 2004; Rubie-Davies et al., 2006; Solomon et al., 1996). As Gregory and Huang (2013) note, "it cannot be ruled out" that implicit bias is at play here (p. 52).

Fiarman (2016) suggests that the first step to addressing unconscious bias is to "eliminate the stigma around talking about our bias" and to "normalize" talking about it. It can help to understand that "unconscious bias is not deliberate; it doesn't reflect our goals and intentions" (para. 9). The process of normalizing bias would include "naming it" in ourselves and others. As uncomfortable as this might be, Fiarman (2016) suggests a few questions that could be helpful:

- What makes you think that? What leads you to that conclusion?
- Would this decision be different if the family/child were of a different race or background?
- How would you make this decision if this were your own child? (para. 14)

Fiarman (2016) recommends three steps for addressing implicit bias: anticipating bias and creating systems to reduce it, building empathy, and holding ourselves accountable. "Deconstructing our unconscious bias takes consistent work," she reminds us. "We can't address it once and be done. We need to recognize these unwanted, deep-rooted beliefs and limit their influence on us. Then our actions will match our intentions" (para. 38).

 ## Using the Life Preserver: Connecting the Contemplative Practice to the Three Tenets

As you'll recall, the Predict, Plan For, and Respond phases of the Contemplative Practice are intended to become a habit of mind that entails inquiry, analysis, and action. Figure 6.5 shows questions designed to guide the Contemplative Practice that are aligned to the tenets of trusting students' intentions, developing students' self-efficacy and agency, and facilitating joy-filled learning.

FIGURE 6.5

Contemplative Practice for Trusting Each Student's Intentions, Developing Each Student's Self-Efficacy and Agency, and Facilitating Joy-Filled Learning

Predict	
(Investigate and Interpret Available Information)	

Questions About My Students	• How does each student see themselves as learners?
	  – Who sees themselves as a capable learner? Who doesn't?
	  – Who is cognizant of their strengths and assets? Who isn't?
	  – Who is free from the harm of stereotypes and implicit bias? Who isn't?
	• How does each student embrace their power as a learner?
	  – Who co-creates our physical, curricular, instructional, and relational spaces? Who doesn't?
	  – Who believes their voice is heard? Who doesn't?
	  – Who believes they make unique contributions to our classroom? Who doesn't?
	  – Who feels confident in making their choices? Who doesn't?

Questions About My Students —(continued)	• How does each student experience joy-filled learning? – Who makes authentic meaning of their learning? Who doesn't? – Who can embrace their purpose for learning? Who can't? – Who can connect to their peers and to me? Who can't? – Who feels intellectually, socially, and emotionally fulfilled? Who doesn't?
Questions About Me and My Actions	• What are my strengths in relationship to trusting student intentions, developing each student's self-efficacy and agency, and facilitating joy-filled learning? • How do I know that what I've investigated about my students' experiences is accurate? • What actions have I taken to honor each student's intentions, self-efficacy, and agency? • What actions have I taken to honor each student's pursuit of joy-filled learning? • What actions have I taken to develop strong relationships that safeguard each student's dignity and ensure a community free of the negative impacts of stereotyping? • What actions have I taken to honor each student's voice and their unique contributions as co-creators of the physical, curricular, instructional, and relational spaces? • What actions have I taken to withhold any of the tenets of community from any student to date? • What actions or inactions on my part may have been counterproductive, destructive, or threatening to each student with regard to trusting student intentions, developing each student's self-efficacy and agency, and facilitating joy-filled learning? • How, if at all, am I responding to barriers I am facing in trusting student intentions, developing each student's self-efficacy and agency, and facilitating joy-filled learning?
Questions to Surface, Interrogate, and Define My Mental Models	• What might it mean to understand learning from the lens of each of my students? • What are my current beliefs about trusting each student's innate desire to learn and grow? • What are my current beliefs about fostering each student's self-efficacy and agency? • What are my current beliefs about facilitating joy-filled learning for each of my students? • What stereotypes or biases have I surfaced in myself about my students' intentions, self-efficacy, or agency? • What stereotypes or biases have I surfaced in myself about my students as joyful learners? • Upon what are these beliefs or biases based? • What data, if any, refutes my beliefs or biases? • How might my beliefs and biases be creating barriers to trusting student intentions, developing each student's self-efficacy and agency, and facilitating joy-filled learning?

(continued)

FIGURE 6.5

Contemplative Practice for Trusting Each Student's Intentions, Developing Each Student's Self-Efficacy and Agency, and Facilitating Joy-Filled Learning—(*continued*)

Plan For (Leverage Strengths to Pinpoint Most Effective Means)	
Questions About Our Way of Being	• Given what I know about my strengths and the strengths of my students, what navigational instruments will I use to trust each student's innate intention to do well, develop each student's self-efficacy and agency, and facilitate joy-filled learning?
Questions About Our Way of Knowing	• How will I use the knowledge I have gained relative to an ethic of hospitality, cultural humility, and equity through dignity and belonging to trust each student's innate intention to do well, develop each student's self-efficacy and agency, and facilitate joy-filled learning? • How will I use the knowledge I possess and other expertise to trust each student's innate intention to do well, develop each student's self-efficacy and agency, and facilitate joy-filled learning?
Questions About Our Way of Thinking	• How will I use questions from each phase of the Contemplative Practice to trust each student's innate intention to do well, develop each student's self-efficacy and agency, and facilitate joy-filled learning? • How effectively have I surfaced my mental models to trust students' innate intention to do well, develop students' self-efficacy and agency, and facilitate joy-filled learning? • What is my plan of action? • Why do I believe this is the best course of action?
Respond (Position Thinking into Responsive Action)	
Questions About My Plan	• When am I going to put my plan into action? • What do I need to do to get ready to execute my plan? • What help do I need and from whom can I get that help? • What resources do I need and how will I acquire those resources? • How do I document my plan's impact as I execute my plan?
Questions About the Results of My Plan	• What worked and how did I know? • What did not work and how did I know? • What will I do more, differently, or better next time? • How will I continue to increase my capacity to extend the tenets of community to each student?

Questions to Resurface, Reinterrogate, and Redefine My Mental Models	• What were my mental models (images, assumptions, beliefs) related to trusting each student's innate intention to do well, developing each student's self-efficacy and agency, and facilitating joy-filled learning? • How, if at all, were my mental models challenged in the process of doing the work? • How, if at all, were my mental models changed? • How, if at all, were these changes beneficial?

We are now ready to disembark at our next three ports of call to observe two more PSC captains in action. Here you will meet two middle school students, 5th grader Myles and 8th grader Willow, and their respective teachers, Jack Campbell and Nichelle Hill-Edwards. You will have the opportunity to see how these teachers extend not only the last three tenets of community, but also the tenets of welcoming and valuing.

PSC Captain Jack Campbell and Myles

Joy, feeling one's own value, being appreciated and loved by others, feeling useful and capable of production are all factors of enormous value to the human soul.

—Maria Montessori

Eleven-year-old Myles is a Black 5th grader in a mid-sized suburban school district. Myles is kind and charismatic, and many adults would call him charming. He easily makes friends with both peers and adults. He can win you over with his big brown eyes and infectious, playful smile, or he can make you feel sorry for him when he hits you with a sad pout. Myles knows how to connect with others and values his ability to be center stage. His sense of humor and wit are magnetic.

Initially, Myles is really excited about starting middle school. He is ready to leave the little kids behind and looking forward to a new beginning. Over the summer, he'd heard that he would have the new 5th grade teacher, Mr. Campbell. He is pumped—people say Mr. Campbell is young, energetic, and "tite." And when Myles finally meets him, everything that he's heard is confirmed. Mr. Campbell is "off the hook." So, Myles starts the school year looking forward to being in class every day. Mr. Campbell seems genuinely happy to see everyone, and being in that classroom just feels good to Myles, who attributes much of his comfort to his amazing new teacher. Terina and Major, Myles's parents, are very pleased about his enthusiasm and are looking forward to opportunities to get to know and work with Mr. Campbell throughout the school year.

During the first month of the school year, Myles is in Mr. Campbell's room all day except for physical education, music, and art. Once everyone is settled in for the school year, he starts going to a different teacher for science but still has Mr. Campbell for social studies. In this middle school, two 5th grade teachers are paired, with one responsible for teaching both sections of science and the other for teaching both sections of social studies. Classes are self-contained for English language arts and math. Jack's teaching partner, Mark Harris, is a veteran teacher who has been in this middle school for about 20 years. The principal paired them hoping that some of Jack's enthusiasm and energy for building relationships with all his kids might rub off a little on Mark.

It isn't long after the science and social studies classes start that Myles realizes the work has started to pile up. He still loves being in Mr. Campbell's room, but he doesn't love doing schoolwork any more than he did in elementary school. He isn't a huge fan of many of his other teachers. They're fine—they just aren't like Mr. Campbell, who he really likes (and who, he's pretty sure, likes him, too). At least Mr. Campbell doesn't treat him like he's dumb. He really hated some of his experiences in elementary school and is hoping not to repeat them in middle school. Then he lands in Mr. Harris's classroom, and everything he dreads about being thought of as dumb by white teachers seems to come to fruition. At least he's only there for an hour a day. Maybe he'll survive.

For his part, Jack is having a great time. As a young, gay, white male professional, he is so happy to have recently moved to this thriving community and to work in this diverse school. He had never before had the opportunity to interact with so many kids from so many different backgrounds. He loves learning about each student, and he is sincerely pleased with the relationships he is building. He gets the sense that his students are happy to be in his classroom. He is conscious of maintaining high expectations while building relationships and connecting with each of his students. He hopes this isn't just the honeymoon period.

As the school year progresses, Jack becomes increasingly concerned about Myles's academic readiness. On the surface, Myles seems connected, comfortable, and content in his classroom. He is an incredibly personable, dynamic young man. But he just isn't progressing as Jack would like. His classwork is erratic, and what little homework Jack assigns often comes back incomplete. When he spoke to Terina and Major at Open House, they indicated that this pattern began in elementary school and that they're working very hard at home to support Myles, but it's difficult. He's a great kid; he just doesn't like to read and doesn't like to do schoolwork.

A few weeks into the year, the entire 5th grade class takes the NWEA test in reading, language, and math. Myles is just above the 50th percentile in math and slightly below the national median in reading and language. He is certainly capable of doing better than he is doing in school. Jack intends to meet with each student to set goals and is anxious to see how he might support a course correction for Myles. But it is still early in the fall, and there is plenty of time for him to help Myles shape up by the end of the year.

As the winter holidays approach, Jack remains concerned about Myles. He certainly isn't failing, but he isn't doing as well as he ought to be doing. Although they did meet to set goals, he definitely isn't showing the growth that Jack wants to see. Myles isn't defiant; he doesn't challenge Jack or refuse any of Jack's requests. He just seems to quietly glide through class, exerting as little effort as he can get away with.

One Sunday afternoon when Jack is at home preparing his lesson plans for the upcoming week, he finds himself struggling to move Myles forward. He had thought he was building a great relationship with him, but in the last several conversations, he just doesn't seem to be getting anywhere. Myles is compliant, respectful, and seemingly very connected to Jack, but their last few serious conversations haven't gone anywhere.

He had asked Myles questions to ascertain whether he felt a sense of belonging in the classroom, as though he was listened to and important. In all cases, Myles indicated that yes, in Jack's room, he felt all those things. When asked if the work was too difficult for him, Myles said no. But when asked what was preventing him from getting some of his work done, he just said, "I don't know." When Jack asked Myles how he could help him, again he replied, "I don't know."

Jack has been emailing with Myles's mother, who confirms that Myles loves being in his classroom. She again mentions that his reluctance to complete his work started in elementary school. She and Major had tried several different things with his teachers, but they never worked. Jack is worried. He doesn't want this habit to continue, and he needs to figure out the best way to help Myles learn and grow as he knows he is capable of doing. Though he has other students who struggle far more than Myles, he's got a plan for each of them, and those plans are working.

The fact that Jack is also seriously displeased with his teaching partner, Mark, isn't helping the situation. At last week's planning meeting, they were reviewing data from the science and social studies classes. Myles is currently failing in science, and Mark has decided that Myles is the type of student who doesn't care about learning or his future. Mark thinks of him as just an unmotivated kid who takes up space and vows not to care about Myles's success more than Myles does himself.

Jack's Use of the Contemplative Practice

Using the questions from Figure 6.5 (p. 110) as a springboard, Jack generates a list of questions unique to Myles (see Figure 6.6).

 Jack Predicts

Jack sits at his dining room table looking at all his notes. He has generated some really good questions to help him think about Myles, and now he is trying to sort through all the details to prioritize his thoughts and focus on what is most important. He leans back and runs his fingers through his hair as he reflects on all he has learned.

FIGURE 6.6

Contemplating the Tenets of Community for Myles

Trusting Each Student's Intentions, Developing Each Student's Self-Efficacy and Agency, and Facilitating Joy-Filled Learning
Questions About Myles

• Who is Myles?
   – What are his dreams and aspirations?
   – Do I know him well enough to know what he loves?
   – What makes him sad?
   – What makes him happy?
   – What is he afraid of?
 	
• What is Myles experiencing?
   – How does Myles see himself as a learner?
   – Does he see his strengths?
   – How does he define his struggles or his apathy toward certain tasks?
   – How does he feel about failing science?
   – How does Myles embrace his power to co-create learning? Does he experience that power in our classroom? What about his science class?
   – To what extent does Myles find relevance and joy in his learning?
   – Does he value what he is learning?
   – How does he connect what he's learning to his life, his future, and his dreams?
   – How does he interact with his peers?
   – How do his peers interact with him?
   – How does Myles describe his experiences in our classroom?
   – How does Myles describe his experiences in other classrooms?
   – What were his experiences like in grades K–4?
   – What experiences at school extend welcoming and valuing to Myles?
   – What experiences destroy or diminish his ability to feel welcomed and valued?
   – Where and how has Myles experienced learning that is free from the barriers that are incompatible with the five tenets?

Questions About Me and My Actions
• How am I demonstrating my trust in Myles's intentions to do well? • What am I doing to build and strengthen his self-efficacy and agency? • How does he interpret my actions to nurture his self-efficacy and agency? • How have my actions safeguarded or diminished Myles's capacity as a learner? • What actions have I taken that withhold any of the tenets from Myles? • How do I respond to Mark's actions? • How am I using my strengths to extend the tenets to Myles? • What do I need to do to support Mark in doing the same?
Questions to Surface, Interrogate, and Define My Mental Models
• Do I have a good enough understanding of what it means to be a young Black male student? • Is my understanding based on truth or is it based on stereotypes and other misinformation? How do I know? • What do I need to learn more about to better understand the young Black male student experience and Myles's experience in particular?

Jack can't get his mind off his conversation with Terina, Myles's mother. It had gone well; Terina was pleased he had called, and she said she was impressed with the level of care with which Jack was approaching his work with her son. Jack asked her what Myles's experience at the elementary school was like, and Terina confirmed that it was as he'd expected. He'd gotten along well with his classmates and teachers. This pattern of underachieving began in 2nd grade. His teachers tried to get him to work harder, but it had always been a struggle.

"Everyone loves Myles, they always said," Terina said.

"Mrs. Stevenson, when you think about Myles—who's a great kid, by the way—what keeps you awake at night?" Jack had asked her.

"Mr. Campbell, that's such an interesting question. I don't think anyone has ever asked me something like that."

"I apologize. I'm not trying to be rude; I just want to understand you and Major as parents—to connect with what you think is important so we can support Myles together."

"Oh, Mr. Campbell, I'm not mad. I'm touched. No one from the school has ever asked me a question like that. Whenever anyone calls from the school, we only talk about what Myles isn't doing that they want him to do. He's never really in trouble; they just always want him to do something, and of course, they want us to help make sure he does it. But no one has ever asked me questions like *What do I worry about?*

"Hmmm. First, I worry about his safety. I don't know a Black mother today who doesn't worry about the safety of her children, especially her boys. I worry every time he walks out that front door when either his father or I am not with him. I guess I worry about him being happy and feeling loved. He knows we love him. I want him to know that others love him, too. I want the world to embrace him as someone special with gifts to share and not as someone to fear, to mistrust, or to look down upon. And I guess I worry about him striving for all that I know he can do. We want him to finish high school, go to college, and find his way in this world. We do not want him to be just another statistic. That's what I worry about, Mr. Campbell. We talk about this all the time."

Why hadn't anyone tried to connect with Myles's parents in ways other than talking about what he wasn't doing at school? Jack wonders if this is a significant part of the story. He sifts through the papers on the table until he finds one from Myles. Jack had used the Student Product Tool (see Appendix G, p. 173), one of the protocols from Powerful Student Care geared toward better understanding what students experience. It's a drawing depicting Myles in the center of the room with stuff coming at him from all directions: comments from teachers and parents, homework assignments, classroom instructions, even quotes from Jack. Myles is holding a shield like a superhero, deflecting all these demands.

Jack remains unsure how to deal with Mark. He is disappointed in himself because he hasn't challenged Mark, but he is new and still trying to find his way with his colleagues. He doesn't think making Mark an enemy will help Myles, and he worries he might brand himself as some kind of radical. Still, he can't help but think that Mark is biased toward Myles. "Does Mark do well only with kids who do everything he asks?" he wonders. "Or only with kids who are white?" Mark doesn't know Myles at all. He can't connect with him; he doesn't *want* to connect with him. How can he possibly help Myles learn? He has no way to activate what Myles knows about any given topic. How can Myles learn from him? Does Mark think his job is just to present content to children and write off those students who don't respond?

Jack turns to his computer and generates a list of what he considers to be the most important issues regarding Myles:

1. Myles has told him he feels welcomed, seen, heard, and valued in his classroom. He hasn't used those exact words, but he's made that point. He doesn't feel the same way in other classes, which Myles says makes him feel like he did when he was in elementary school.

2. Jack infers from his conversation with Terina that no one at the elementary school interacted with Myles's parents unless they wanted to complain about something Myles wasn't doing. Myles doesn't have any behavior problems. He just doesn't always do what is asked of him, especially when it comes to academics.

3. In his drawing, Myles seems to put himself on the defensive. Everyone is barking out work, instructions, and commands from which he is trying to shield himself. It doesn't look like Myles is in control in the drawing. Everything is aimed in a single direction, from somewhere else, straight at him. He seems to feel powerless.

4. Jack isn't trying to make too many assumptions about other teachers, but it seems that they've had low expectations for Myles since elementary school. He hasn't strived to achieve; he hasn't always done his work. He has often been placed in the lower reading groups. Myles's casual approach to his learning has continued into 5th grade. Is Myles responding to a history of low expectations? Is he becoming a statistic because of how we have been treating him? Is he responding to what he hears "the world" say about Black boys and Black men? It seems Myles is already carrying the weight of the world on his young shoulders.

5. And the hardest question of all: How is he using his connection with Myles to share power with him and to help Myles see his trust and confidence in him rather than disappointment?

 ## Jack Plans

While Jack is pretty confident that Myles feels welcomed and valued in his classroom, it is becoming increasingly obvious that he has yet to experience the other three tenets. How can he possibly think that we trust his innate intentions to do well, that we want him to experience a level of self-confidence and power as a co-creator of his learning, or that he can feel joy because he sees purpose and relevance in what and how he learns? Everything is being done *to* him, not with him—and his teachers have been focused on what he's *not* doing instead of what he could be doing.

"I'm guilty too," Jack thinks to himself. "I took his NWEA results, noted that they show more understanding than he shows in class, and constructed a plan to fix a deficiency. I've been perpetuating the issue and I've failed to look at it through Myles's lens rather than my own."

Jack had had the very best of intentions when he spoke to Myles about his NWEA growth goals. All he had wanted was for Myles to succeed. But he hadn't really listened to Myles. He hadn't really asked Myles for his take. Myles likely didn't think there was a problem. Jack had identified a problem from only his perspective and had tried to quickly solve it in his way, so he could move on to the next student's problem to solve. Inadvertently, he was reinforcing Myles's elementary experience. The only reason Myles is doing as well as he is in Jack's class is because they have a good relationship. But Jack hasn't been listening as carefully as he needs to, and he hasn't taken into consideration Myles's perspective.

Myles views himself as having little or no power to influence his learning. Through power sharing, Jack wants Myles to develop self-efficacy and experience agency. Jack also wants Myles to know that he is confident in Myles's ability to make good choices and that Myles can become confident and optimistic about it, too. Using the inquiry-based instructional model and giving Myles the chance to learn about something that matters to him and to share his learning with his peers, with Jack, and with his parents might be the key to getting Myles excited about learning and enabling him to build his self-confidence.

Sitting in his dining room, Jack finds it all starting to make sense. He is going to plot a new course and invite Myles on the journey. In fact, he will invite Myles to lead the way. Jack decides upon the following courses of action:

1. He will modify the curriculum for Myles by inviting him to explore a topic that means something to him. Myles's biggest struggle is with reading. He seems uninterested in developing his reading skills. Even when he was involved in a drama production, it was hard to get him interested in reading. He doesn't have a learning disability; he just isn't motivated. Jack can work on developing Myles's reading skills within the context of his exploration. Myles needs to see the power in what he learns in a way that matters to him.

2. Once Myles and Jack negotiate the subject of his exploration, they can co-create a process for learning. Together, they can

determine milestones and a format for progress conferences that Myles will need. They can also decide how often Jack will give Myles feedback and what mini-lessons will look like. He might guide Myles in regularly and routinely reporting the progress of his exploration to his parents and ask Myles to determine how to involve Jack in that process.

Jack thinks he is probably "overdoing" the power sharing a bit, but he wants Myles to feel like he's in the driver's seat. He wants to shift classroom instruction from what Myles perceives as being done to him or at him to what he hopes Myles will interpret as his opportunity to prove to himself and to others that he is completely capable and ready to soar. He wants Myles to love learning, to feel good about himself, and to feel confident in his ability to learn. Jack will also use this curriculum modification as a pilot for using more inquiry-based approaches with all his students.

3. Jack will invite Myles to become a playwright. Getting Myles to write will be a great way to fortify his reading skills. When students read what they write, they often are more fluent and enjoy the experience more. Perhaps Myles's plays can even be staged in drama class or after school. Myles can act in or co-direct these productions. These activities might help Myles develop a sense of self-efficacy and agency as he "hosts" others' learning through them.

4. Jack will increase his use of cooperative learning. Given that Myles is so social, perhaps this strategy will increase his motivation.

5. Finally, Jack will engage in student-led goal setting with a small group of students that includes Myles. This group of students can function as a leadership team of sorts piloting the use of student-led goal setting and conferencing. This will give Myles another chance to develop self-efficacy and agency and to have a voice in his learning experiences.

Jack can't wait to talk to Myles. He is pretty confident that this change in approach will be just what Myles needs to feel differently about learning.

Jack Responds

Jack has his plan. He recognizes not only the importance of opening the world of knowledge to Myles, but also the need for Myles to shape that world. Jack hasn't used the inquiry-based learning instructional model enough to be confident in what he is going to attempt with Myles. But it makes enough sense (not just for Myles, but for many of his students) for him to give it a go. He decides to plan inquiry-based units of instruction, starting on a small scale.

Jack isn't concerned about perfection in his use of this curricular and instructional model. It is an experiment. He's a good teacher; he can make it work. What really matters and what he really wants to see is how Myles will respond to the new opportunities and how his perception of himself as a learner will change over time. Jack will also speak to Myles's parents and ask them to note any comments he makes at home that reflect changes in how he sees his experience at school and himself as a learner. That feedback could prove to be invaluable information moving forward.

Jack has taken several workshops related to Powerful Student Care. He is deeply committed to proving to each student that they are distinctive and irreplaceable. He finds the five tenets to be powerful for really changing students' experiences in classrooms, and he is particularly intrigued with the exploration of mental models as part of the Contemplative Practice.

In recalling several conversations he has had with friends about their own K–12 experiences, Jack notes that they would talk about friends, relationships, extracurricular activities, sometimes a teacher or other adult, but seldom about the place where they had spent the vast majority of their time at school: their classrooms.

Jack hopes that aligning with the last three tenets of community will help Myles experience academic learning as joy, which he is sure Myles has rarely, if ever, done. Experiencing the joy of learning feeds the human drive to grow and to do well. Myles has shown Jack just how important it is for each student to feel welcomed and valued as a human being in the classroom and as a part of a community of difference. But he has also shown him that feeling welcomed and valued alone is not enough.

Jack believes in Myles's desire to do well even though this can be hard to discern because he has carefully hidden it away. As he thinks about trusting Myles's innate intention to do well, he knows that Myles will be a lot happier and more self-assured if he thinks of himself as a capable learner who recognizes his own strengths. Structuring successful experiences for Myles means letting him have input into creating his curricular and instructional spaces so he can explore ideas and content that are relevant to his life, his dreams, and the world around him.

Jack has always been able to build relationships with kids. He has this innate ability to show them how important they are and how glad he is that they are in his classroom. Now he better understands dignity-conscious relationships, the power of sharing his classroom with his students, and what it means to see each one of them as a co-creator of teaching and learning.

Jack is haunted by Terina's fears for her child's safety. He knows that his plans for Myles won't change the formidable negative forces he will face as a Black man in our society. Nonetheless, it is his responsibility to help Myles see his capacity as a learner, use his own voice, and steadfastly pursue his dreams.

PSC Captain Nichelle Hill-Edwards and Willow

The greatness of humanity is not in being human, but in being humane.

—Mahatma Gandhi

Willow's 8th grade year has started on a great note, and she is very excited about being in her last year in middle school. She thinks her classes are going to be fun, and she is happy with most of her teachers. What she's most excited about, though, is her math teacher. She can't believe that one of her teachers is a doctor. She's never met a Black female doctor before except during medical appointments, and she thinks it's really cool to have one as a math teacher.

Willow, who is 14, was born Sofia Victoria Serrano in Mexico. When her family arrived in the United States six years ago, none of them spoke English. She and her siblings were immediately placed in their school district's ELL program. Today, having been well served by the ELL program and its dedicated teachers, Willow is fluent in English and no longer accesses the second-language services. She was thrilled to exit the ELL program at the end of her 7th grade year, having felt stigmatized and embarrassed by being in the pull-out program. Throughout the early months of the school year, Willow and her math teacher, Nichelle Hill-Edwards, have developed a strong relationship. They have had great conversations, and Nichelle really feels like she's getting to know this young lady.

Nichelle is excited today because it's the day she is launching her annual mentoring program. Many students show up after school to hear more about the club, commit to the work, and get started with training. Nichelle began Project Soar about three years ago with the goal of pairing an 8th grader with a 5th grader as a way of acclimating 5th graders to the middle school. Eighth grade students serve as peer mentors to help incoming 5th graders navigate the middle school system and help them feel that they are an important part of the school.

This year, Nichelle is partnering with the new 5th grade teacher, Jack Campbell. She has about 20 students beginning the training this afternoon. She is hoping to recruit a few more students, which would enable her to pair an 8th grade partner with every student in Jack's class. But as happy as she is about the prospects for this year's group, she is also disappointed that her student Willow, who had expressed interest in the program, never shows up for training.

Nichelle thinks about how bright and talented Willow is. She recalls the time she asked Willow about her nickname. Willow told her she had chosen that name when she was in 5th grade after hearing it on TV and thinking it sounded really American. When Nichelle probed a bit further, Willow told her how awful it felt when people stared at her for being called out of class to go learn English because she couldn't speak like everyone else. Some students even made comments and laughed at her. Worse yet, Willow believes that many people just don't like her because she was born in another country. She fears that some people want her to be arrested and to be sent back to Mexico. Nichelle keeps hearing Willow's last comment replaying in her head: "Not everyone is happy that people like me are here. My sister Mia was born here; she's an American. I'm not. It's just easier to be Willow. I don't want to be sent away. I want to be here."

Nichelle is trying to better understand what is happening in Willow's world. Clearly, she has been on the receiving end of some racist and xenophobic comments from peers. Though middle school kids are often unkind, Nichelle considers these comments to be more than just middle school behavior. Willow had been doing really well in her classes until mid-October, when the entire 8th grade participated in the career fair. Nichelle tries to recall which sessions Willow attended, but can't be sure. It was around this time that Willow's work habits started to change. The changes were slight in Nichelle's classroom, but more noticeable in Willow's other classes. As the weeks continued, her other teachers said she had checked out. She wasn't turning in homework. She was quiet in class, and she seemed apathetic. But she was very polite. She followed the rules and didn't cause her teachers any problems.

Nichelle remembers the disagreement she had with the middle school counselor, Liz, when she saw Willow's name wasn't on the list to meet with college representatives. Early in the 8th grade year, the counselors and teachers tried to connect as many students as possible with the college representatives who visited the school to get kids excited about higher education, think about what colleges are looking for in prospective students, and consider what they would need to do in high school to be as prepared as possible.

Liz said she hadn't invited Willow because she'd been in an ELL program last year and Liz's practice was not to invite students in support programs to meet with college representatives. "Most of those students go to the community college if they go at all," she told Nichelle. Nichelle was aghast, and the more she talked with Liz, the angrier she became.

The changes in Willow's coursework and demeanor grew even starker from that point on. Willow seemed to avoid making eye contact with Nichelle and had begun to rack up missing assignments in her class.

By the time Project Soar was ready to begin, Nichelle thought this chance to mentor a younger student was exactly what Willow needed to reconnect and reenergize. She thought Willow was on board and even excited to be a mentor. Nichelle realizes she will need to dig deeper if she is going to really understand what is happening in Willow's mind, heart, and world. She needs to get started right away. Willow doesn't have any more time to lose.

Nichelle's Use of the Contemplative Practice

Nichelle has embraced the Powerful Student Care training she received last year. In particular, she appreciates the use of inquiry and the Contemplative Practice, which she finds helps her to ask good questions, seek answers, and formulate a plan. She uses the Quick View Tool in Appendix C (p. 163) to connect all the key components she needs to consider, including tenets, barriers to tenets, bodies of knowledge, navigational instruments, and so on.

Using the questions in Figure 6.5 (p. 110) as a springboard, Nichelle generates a list of questions unique to Willow to support her in the Contemplative Practice (see Figure 6.7, p. 128).

 Nichelle Predicts

Nichelle can't decide if she is more frustrated with Willow for not engaging with Project Soar or with herself for not knowing more about what is going on with Willow. She is trying to recall one of the conversations she had with Willow's mother. It had been awkward because of the language barrier, but if she remembers correctly, Willow had enjoyed the career fair. Nothing seemed to be out of order, so why did Willow seem to quickly spiral downward after that event? It doesn't make any sense. Nichelle knows she needs to have another conversation with Liz. She also needs to email her 8th grade colleagues and ask them for advice. She wants to speak with Willow's mother again and to have another conversation with Willow, too.

It's been a whirlwind of a week. Willow's demeanor hasn't changed much in the classroom, though she is now trying to avoid eye contact with Nichelle. During her planning period, Nichelle quickly assembles her notes on Willow and has another conversation with Liz.

"I've only heard from Willow once this entire year," Liz says. "It was right after the career fair, when she stopped in and asked if she

FIGURE 6.7

Contemplating the Tenets of Community for Willow

Trusting Each Student's Intentions, Developing Each Student's Self-Efficacy and Agency, and Facilitating Joy-Filled Learning
Questions About Willow

- Who is Willow?
  - What are her dreams and aspirations?
  - Do I know her well enough to know what she loves?
  - What makes her sad?
  - What makes her happy?
  - What is she afraid of?

- What is Willow experiencing?
  - How does Willow see herself as a learner?
  - Does she see her strengths?
  - How does she define her struggles or her apathy toward certain tasks?
  - Where does this growing apathy come from?
  - Why is Willow more eager to learn in my classroom than in other classrooms? What are the variables?
  - How does Willow embrace her power to co-create learning? Does she experience that power in my classroom? What about other classrooms?
  - How did Willow experience the career fair? Why might this be one of the catalysts for the change in her demeanor?
  - To what extent does Willow find relevance and joy in her learning?
  - Does she value what she is learning?
  - How does she connect what she's learning to her life? To her future? To her dreams?
  - How does she interact with her peers?
  - How do her peers interact with her?
  - How does Willow think about her experiences in my classroom versus in other classrooms?
  - What experiences at school extend welcoming and valuing to Willow?
  - What experiences destroy or diminish her ability to feel welcomed and valued?
  - What impact does Liz's bias have on Willow? Is Willow aware of it? If so, what is her reaction to it? Is she experiencing this perceived limitation on her potential from others as well?
  - Where and how has Willow experienced learning that is free from barriers to the tenets?

Questions About Me and My Actions

- How am I demonstrating my trust in Willow's intentions to do well?
- What am I doing to build and strengthen her self-efficacy and agency?
- How does she interpret my actions to nurture her self-efficacy and agency?
- How have my actions safeguarded or diminished Willow's capacity as a learner?
- What actions have I or others taken that withhold any of the tenets from Willow?
- How am I using my strengths to extend the tenets to Willow? What do I need to do to support others in doing the same?
- How am I going to respond to the barriers Liz puts in Willow's way?

Questions to Surface, Interrogate, and Define My Mental Models
• Do I have a good enough understanding of what it means to be a young Latina? To be an English language learner? To be an immigrant trying to feel at home in a new country?   • Is my understanding based on truth, or is it based on stereotypes and other misinformation?   • What do I need to learn more about to better understand what Willow is experiencing?

could be on the list to see the university reps. I told her that wouldn't be possible."

"What do you mean, you told her it wasn't possible? Why not?"

"Like I told you the last time we talked, I don't invite students from the ELL program. They go to the community college. Besides, Willow's family doesn't have the means to send her to the university. Why should she see the reps when it isn't possible for her to attend college? Isn't that cruel, Nichelle?"

"What's cruel, Liz, is you shutting her down and telling her she can't do something. Why would you do something like that? Who knows what can happen? We don't know that Willow won't earn scholarships to help her afford school. I didn't even realize that was a goal of hers."

"Well, we don't know if she will meet all the criteria for scholarships and assistance, so I think it's completely out of her reach. She needs to consider what other people like her do. Some of them, the really ambitious ones, go to the local community college and they do just fine there."

"I'm trying to understand what you're saying without actually saying it, Liz. I'm pretty shocked and pretty angry right now and I'm trying to find the right words to—"

"You can stop right, there, Dr. Hill-Edwards. I do this work every day, not you. This girl comes into my office with unrealistic plans. She's not doing well in her classes, if you look at her grades, and she comes into my office asking about Washington State University. I mean, come on. Let's get a grip on reality. Not inviting her to see the university reps is just a good dose of truth. Maybe she'll start to consider her valid options."

"She's in 8th grade, Liz!"

Nichelle leaves Liz's office thinking two confrontational and unproductive conversations with this counselor are just about all she can process right now. She needs to support Willow, and she needs something to be done about Liz's biased and prejudicial way of crushing certain kids' dreams.

Later that week, with the help of an interpreter, Nichelle reaches out again to Willow's mother. Their conversation is warm and friendly, and Nichelle makes clear that she sees strong potential in Willow. Her mother is appreciative. Willow hasn't talked much at home about her classes recently, and Nichelle is the only teacher her parents have heard from.

At one point, Willow's mom says that a group of girls at the school seems to be targeting Willow, who had asked that her mother not do anything or say anything about it. Willow's mother and father are baffled by her seemingly growing disinterest in school. They don't have experience navigating U.S. schools, and they don't know how much of a problem this disengagement in school will be in the long run. They just want Willow to get through the year, and they're hoping that high school might be a better fit for her.

It is not lost on Nichelle that Willow's parents care deeply for their daughter, but they haven't said a word about education after high school. "The plot thickens," Nichelle thinks.

Next, Nichelle reviews responses from her 8th grade colleagues to her email asking for advice. None of them have any idea what the issues are behind her disengagement and apathy. Nichelle gets the feeling that they've all been overlooking Willow. None of them seem interested in engaging in conversation. They don't have many questions and aren't too worried because Willow is kind, sweet, and "not a behavior problem at all." They have accepted her passivity in their classes.

Finally, Nichelle recalls her latest conversation with Willow. At the career fair, Willow told her, she had been told that she looked just like Ana Cabrera, a Mexican American television journalist. Willow wants to follow in Cabrera's footsteps and attend Washington State as she had done. Nichelle also learns that Willow is hesitant to speak with her parents about attending university because she doesn't think they can afford to send her there and doesn't want them to feel badly.

Things are beginning to make sense now. As she puts it all together, Nichelle identifies what she thinks are the big ideas she needs to explore further:

1. Willow wants to follow in the footsteps of a famous and very successful Mexican American journalist. Nichelle had no idea about this.

2. Willow's excitement is not shared by others. She chose not to tell her parents about her desire to be a journalist, instead leading them to believe she is interested in hospitality, as she doesn't believe they can afford to send her to Washington State. The counselor has all but shut down Willow's dream. Liz's biased, unilateral refusal to connect students from the ELL program with college reps is not being countered by anyone at school or at home. Liz has even made assumptions about what Willow's parents might say or not say.

3. Willow works hard to belong. She's trying to figure out who she is and who she wants to become. She is seeking to understand how a young Mexican immigrant fits into U.S. society, and she's doing so on her own, without guidance from adults. Her other teachers' lack of interest in how she's doing confirms in Willow's mind Liz's biased message about college being out of reach.

4. Willow struggles to see herself as capable and talented. Negative messages have damaged her self-confidence and crushed her ability to see the relevance of her learning to live her own life and dreams. Her teachers haven't done what's needed to make that relevance clear.

5. Willow has always revered Nichelle's status as a doctor. As a woman of color, Nichelle demonstrates to her what is possible. However, Nichelle understands that she comes from a position of privilege relative to Willow. She is not an immigrant, and she comes from a middle-class family with college-educated parents. Although Willow's story is different from hers, Nichelle

can help her see what she doesn't yet see to continue in her journey. She concedes that she hasn't nurtured Willow's self-efficacy and agency as successfully as she thought.

6. Nichelle also realizes that she has not safeguarded Willow's dignity and that doing so has to be a priority moving forward.

Nichelle also decides on some questions to answer:

1. How do I reinvigorate Willow's interest in journalism?
2. What's going on with this group of girls targeting her?
3. Why is she avoiding eye contact with me, and what does that mean?
4. Why doesn't she want to be a part of Project Soar? How can I get her to reconsider that decision?

 ## Nichelle Plans

That evening, it only takes Nichelle seconds on the internet to find examples of highly successful female immigrant journalists of color to share with Willow. She needs to show Willow in a tangible way that her dream is possible. She also wants to prove to Willow that she is in her camp.

Their conversation the next day goes well. Willow thanks her for the information about the journalists and seems surprised that Nichelle did all this research for her. Nichelle is also able to confirm some assumptions. Willow feels like not attending college would be a disappointment to someone like Nichelle, and she doesn't want to let her down. During their conversation, Willow agrees to think about participating in Project Soar and says she'll let Nichelle know the next day.

After their talk, Nichelle decides on the following action steps:

1. She will ask one of the high school counselors, Kelly Young, herself an Asian American woman, to meet with Willow and start mentoring her. Kelly is charismatic and outgoing and has done a lot of work supporting immigrant students and families in the community. Kelly has the expertise Willow can benefit from to help her uphold her dream and validate her educational goals.

2. She will implement a series of closing rituals in her classroom to create a stronger sense of community among her students. The tenets are not alive enough in her classroom. She has introduced them, and she talks about them with students regularly, but clearly that is not enough. Taking an idea from Zaretta Hammond's (Rebora, 2021/2022) work in equity and culturally responsive teaching, Nichelle decides to create a closing ritual for each of the five tenets of community. For example, she might engage her students in a brief discussion about the ways in which the lesson demonstrates her trust in their intentions to do well. "How did I help you realize that intention? What did your peers do to support that intention? How did you support your peers?" This closing ritual will provide an opportunity for students to talk about their experiences with at least one of the tenets every single day.

3. She will follow up with Willow and do everything she can to convince her to participate in Project Soar. Willow has a passion for people, and Nichelle thinks it will really boost her self-confidence to mentor younger students.

4. She will work to change Liz's inequitable, discriminatory practices. Though she's not sure how it will happen, policies and procedures need to change so that Liz isn't the only gatekeeper to important programs. Nichelle will start by expressing her concerns to the principal and discussing the situation with colleagues who are likely to be receptive to concerns about equity.

5. She will use a multidisciplinary approach to teach her students how to think critically and talk about the social and political issues that affect their lives while also building their math skills and knowledge. Using appropriate data sources related to issues of interest to students and aligned to the math standards, her students will strengthen both their data literacy and their information literacy skills. They will learn to generate discussion questions and statements about the data sets they study, identify any additional information needed, and determine how to potentially take action related to the issue.

Nichelle Responds

Some of Nichelle's plan is unique to Willow, and other parts of the plan will also be helpful for the other students in her classes. Acting from an ethic of hospitality, her plans to secure a mentor for Willow and to encourage Willow to participate in Project Soar are two ways Nichelle hopes to open the world to Willow. She will help all students to see the relevance and importance of their classes in realizing their aspirations.

Nichelle's goal is for Willow to develop the self-efficacy and agency to discern and disregard feedback that places prejudicial limits on her potential and her aspirations, even when that feedback is offered by adults in positions of authority. She recalls tools she saw in her Powerful Student Care workshops that can help her better understand Willow's experiences: the Student Perspective Survey, Student Conversation Tool, Student Observation Tool, and Student Product Tool (see Appendixes D, E, F, and G on pages 167, 169, 171, and 173).

As Nichelle reflects on the last phase of the Contemplative Practice, she notes several shifts in her thinking. Her perspective has changed in a few important areas. Most obvious to her, she no longer believes that she alone can help a student stay on course. She is deeply committed to building relationships that uphold her students' inherent human dignity, but she had underestimated the power of a single damaging voice. She had also waited way too long to approach Willow, and it was only after Willow had decided not to participate in one of her pet projects that she had begun to ask questions.

In the future, she needs to do a better job of asking the right questions to better understand what her students are facing. She also realizes that she needs to be very explicit in helping students see the relevance of their learning to their lives, their aspirations, and the world around them. Too often she's gotten caught in the standard or the learning target as the goal itself and forgotten to help students find relevance in what they are learning.

At first Nichelle thought it might also be necessary to help Willow engage in a truthful conversation with her parents about her hopes for the future. Although she still thinks it's important for Willow to have that conversation, she also realizes that she doesn't know enough yet to be helpful. She recalls from Powerful Student Care that she needs to practice cultural humility. She needs to learn more about Latin American culture, about immigration issues, and more deeply about what it means to live in both a Latin American culture and the broader U.S. culture. She needs help more deeply understanding this experience so she can respect Willow's cultural identity and better understand her lived experience. Perhaps Kelly Young at the high school can help. She will also reach out to Willow's family to gain a better understanding of their specific experience. She doesn't have a good understanding of what cultural implications there might be or what family issues there might be associated with a young adult going away to college. Getting Willow back on course is more than just getting her to pass her classes. It's about proving to Willow that her path is full of promise.

It's Your Turn!

Identify one student who you believe is not experiencing at least one of the three tenets of community discussed in this chapter.

1. What is the student's name?

2. Which tenet(s) are you concerned the student is not experiencing?
   ☐ Each student is here to do well.
   ☐ Each student is here to develop self-efficacy and agency.
   ☐ Each student is here to experience the joy of learning academically, socially, and emotionally.

3. What questions will you ask yourself in the Predict phase of the Contemplative Practice to interpret all available information?

4. How will you use this information to pinpoint the most effective means of addressing this student's interests and needs in the Plan For phase?

5. How does your plan incorporate an ethic of hospitality, cultural humility, equity through belonging and dignity, and other areas of your expertise as well as the navigational instruments for building community?

6. How will you put your thinking into responsive action?

7

It's Your Turn
to Take the Helm

*All labor that uplifts humanity has dignity and importance and
should be undertaken with painstaking excellence.*

—Dr. Martin Luther King Jr.

In observing Stewart, Meredith, Jack, and Nichelle, you have learned
from captains who are primarily focused on a specific student. But
what does it look like to extend Powerful Student Care to an entire
class? Let's observe a fifth PSC captain as she makes stops at each of
the five ports of call on her journey to The Harbor.

Londyn Dale is an 8th grade English language arts (ELA) teacher.
In this chapter, you will shadow Londyn as she asks questions, seeks
answers, makes decisions, and takes action to provide Powerful Student Care to each of her students.

Meet Londyn

Londyn Dale has had many experiences in her 26-year education
career. She spent most of her career in the elementary classroom
teaching multiple grade levels, but mainly 3rd grade. She also spent
several years in middle school teaching 6th and 7th grades. Londyn

served as the Title I teacher, did some instructional coaching, and served several terms as the teachers' union president. She was often seen as the go-to person at each of her schools.

Recently, Londyn engaged in some significant professional development regarding Powerful Student Care. She has high hopes for the approach, as she's tired of putting Band-Aids on complicated issues. She knows there must be a better way to nurture children and to bring humanity to the endeavor of educating them.

In learning about Powerful Student Care, Londyn surfaced some of her own mental models about children, schooling, teachers, and even the purpose of public education. She has always focused on challenging the status quo to better serve each student, and she is humbled by the task of ensuring that each student knows they are distinctive and irreplaceable.

It's Your Turn! The Educator in the Mirror

We know you may be tempted to skip this part, but we hope you don't. Give yourself a gift. We urge you to take the time to actually write down your answers to the "It's Your Turn!" questions in this chapter. After all, the best strategy for improving your teaching, enhancing the learning environment in your classroom, building richer relationships with students, addressing the challenges you face, and finding greater joy in being an educator is to know yourself.

- Who are you as an educator? What is your story?

- What is your vision for the work you do with children every day?

- How does Powerful Student Care align with your vision?

- If each student knew they were distinctive and irreplaceable and that others were also, how would that impact the world we live in?

Packing Our Bags (Front-Loading)

As the fantastic summer days start ever so slightly to shorten, Londyn becomes keenly aware of the upcoming school year. She's been thinking about it all summer, but now it's time to dive in and get serious about what she's going to do.

As she thinks about the tenets of community, Londyn knows everything she does in the classroom has to be filtered through each of the five PSC tenets. She intends to create a space in her classroom that differs from students' previous classrooms. She hopes to create a "sacred space" where what students feel and experience is her measure of success. Her students will be able to depend on this sacred space to experience belonging, safety, trust, self-efficacy, agency, and learning that is both relevant and joyful. And she can't do it alone: Students will need to build the space with her, to grow with one another, to support one another, and to arrive at a place where they can understand and appreciate what they have accomplished individually and collectively throughout the school year. "It's going to be better for both kids and adults," Londyn thinks. "It will be a more humane situation."

Londyn understands that students must feel welcomed and valued before they can envision success and go after it. In this sacred space, she will capitalize on each student's innate drive to grow. And it will not be a place of wounding: Each student will be freed from stereotyping and bias and ensured equity. This has to be a place where each student feels distinctive and irreplaceable whether or not they are academically successful. It must be a place where one's humanity is more important than the pacing guide, and each kid has to believe it is a space crafted just for them.

Londyn will be working with a wide range of students. Many of them are successful—they know how schooling works, they face few barriers to achievement, and they understand how to connect with their friends and to build camaraderie with their teachers. But Londyn also knows that many other kids are struggling to find their way, to learn, to build the social and emotional skills they will need in school and in life. These students don't feel connected to adults. They don't believe in themselves or think their teachers believe in them.

When students walk into her classroom on the very first day, Londyn wants them to experience something dramatically different from what they'd expected. For this to happen, she knows that many of her practices need to be better aligned to the components of Powerful Student Care. She will begin rethinking how she does things as a teacher and will redesign any practices that prevent her students from experiencing all five of the PSC tenets. To this end, she creates the following list of classroom practices and processes that she will need to revise:

1. She will rethink the balance of power in her classroom. Londyn needs to ensure that her relationships with students reflect the unlimited power of seeing one another as human beings in pursuit of their potential. She wants students to see her potential as their teacher, to travel with them on this journey, and to understand, value, and work toward their potential—not only as students but also as human beings on life's journey.

2. She will rethink her classroom management strategies. Focusing on managing behavior with consequences and rewards is antithetical to the PSC tenets. Powerful Student Care isn't about "managing" kids; it's about creating a sense of community among students by *living* the tenets. The tenets will become the norms of her classroom—a way of being in the sacred space. Before this can happen, she needs to build student understanding of the tenets. Rather than begin the school year with conversations about rules and expectations, she will help students appreciate what the tenets are, what they mean, and how they contribute to a shared sense of community.

3. She will rethink her grading, homework, and classroom-based assessment practices. This sacred space will have to respond

to the innate human drive to do well. Her practices need to promote learning and further growth. She will need to give students multiple chances to show what they can do; time will be the variable, not learning. Students will have a voice in assessing their learning. Londyn wants to avoid using a deficit lens and arouse students' curiosity, give them voice, and foster their autonomy and motivation. She wants grades to reflect what students have learned, not simply what they have done to comply with instructions, and to celebrate and honor students' accomplishments.

4. She will rethink how she communicates with families, helping parents and other stakeholders to understand and appreciate the sacred space and what students will experience in it. She will show them how the space helps their children to reach for their infinite potential and how it will help her support each student.

5. She will use the Contemplative Practice to ensure the sacred space is free from mental models that are incompatible with Powerful Student Care (e.g., stereotyping, othering, violations to dignity, fixed mindsets, transactional teaching and learning, deficit thinking, implicit bias).

It's Your Turn! Preparing the Space

- Londyn refers to what she wants to build in her classroom as a "sacred space." What do you want to create? How would you describe it?

- If your students are going to experience each of the tenets of community, you must eliminate classroom practices that pose a barrier to doing so. What practices will you need to examine?

- In what ways do each of the practices on your list pose a barrier for each student to experience the tenets?

Preparing the Students for Our Destination

With her plan for a sacred space in place, Londyn needs to think about how to begin the school year and how to engage her students in this journey with her. She needs to think about how she will get their attention on the very first day and how she will build on that energy in the first few weeks of school. The first day has to be about first impressions of what they will experience in the classroom. No matter what she does on the first day, each student will be formulating thoughts and opinions about what is going to transpire in the coming year. They'll wonder, is she nice? Will she be kind? Will she want to know me? Will she make an effort to know me? Will I be safe in this room with her? Will she care about me? Will she care enough about me to help me when I need it? Will I be able to talk to her? Can I trust her? Is she going to be mean? Will she not really like me because my other teachers haven't liked me? Am I going to like this class?

Londyn knows that her students will quickly start answering those questions and cementing the answers in stone over the first few days or weeks. First impressions are hard to change. Day one has to be about human connections, and each successive day must be about deepening those connections. First impressions, even good ones, are not relationships. Those take time and require sharing, asking questions, listening, connecting, and learning about one another and ourselves.

Over the course of the first month of school, Londyn plans to embed the following plans into her daily lessons:

1. Establish the priority of ongoing relationship building focused on appreciating and understanding one another's identities and stories.

2. Introduce and develop a shared understanding of each tenet of community.
3. Introduce and continue to build an understanding of the words *distinctive* and *irreplaceable* and how they describe the equal value of each student.
4. Connect all these ideas together with developing a shared commitment to the concept of the sacred space Londyn is co-creating with her students.

It's Your Turn! Engaging Students in the Journey

- How do you typically start your school year? What messages are you sending to your students when you do it this way?

- How compatible are your typical beginning-of-the-year practices with the tenets of community?

- How will you introduce the tenets of community to your students?

- How will you deepen students' understanding of the tenets?

- How will the tenets be the filter for everything you do together?

- What do you want the notion that "each of your students is distinctive and irreplaceable" to mean to your students?

Using the Navigational Instruments and the Sails

Londyn finds it really invigorating to set up the new classroom space. Over the summer, as the contents were moved into the hallway and back in again after deep summer cleaning, it was hard to imagine this physical space as an exciting and welcoming place to be. Londyn recalls the moment she entered the space for the first time. She was struck by its cleanliness and sterility. It was seemingly void of all personality and charm.

Three days later, and it's spectacular! Desks are arranged purposefully for collaboration. Bulletin boards are completed, posters and pictures are hung on the walls, welcome signs and posters featuring the tenets of community are strategically placed. Areas for displaying student work are ready and waiting to celebrate the new students. She will use flexible seating. Students will be allowed to choose where they are most comfortable learning. They will have options—bean bags, tall and short tables, a couch, traditional desks. She has even crafted a spot in one of the corners as a place for one-on-one conversations, just far enough away from everyone else, where she hopes students will be eager to talk to her about themselves and to build relationships with one another. Comfortable chairs, an accent rug, and an end table with photos of Londyn's family make it feel like a corner of her living room rather than a classroom space. She hopes it will feel like home to her students, too.

When Londyn first took inventory of this learning space earlier in the week, she was impressed with the space and its potential— tons of storage, beautiful furniture, lots of space. It was a good-sized room, and she was excited to get the transformation underway. There were two large four-drawer filing cabinets in the corner behind the teacher's desk. Both of them were full. After rummaging through the files for a little over an hour, she discovered that her predecessor had used these cabinets to store handouts, assessments, worksheets, and various other instructional materials. In fact, it appeared the entire year was laid out for her in these eight drawers. She remembered that the idea of teaching as transactional is incompatible with Powerful

Student Care. These materials would have to go. She decided to keep the resources she *might* use in one of the cabinets and just slipped the others into the hallway. Perhaps someone else needed them.

Londyn knows that the idea of co-creating a community with her students is essential to the provision of Powerful Student Care. As she learns more about her students, she will draw upon the three theoretical foundations (the vertical threads of the sails) and her own expertise (the horizontal threads) to co-create a sense of community not only through the physical space, but also through the curricular, instructional, and relational/cultural spaces. And she will use the PSC navigational instruments to guide her. In every aspect of her pedagogy, she needs to keep these elements of PSC at the forefront of her mind.

At first, pulling all the elements of Powerful Student Care together seems like it will be a challenge, but Londyn finds the Quick View Tool (Appendix C, p. 163) helps her keep track of everything. In fact, rather than feeling overwhelmed by the idea of providing Powerful Student Care, she has come to appreciate how much it's refocused her thinking on just five tenets that serve as a guide for virtually everything else she needs to do. The PSC framework has also moved her thinking away from a focus on addressing kids' needs based on the services for which they are eligible and the labels they are given to a focus on their humanity above all else.

Londyn thinks about one of the navigational instruments of Powerful Student Care: structures, processes, routines, and rituals. She has read about Jeffrey Benson's (2021) closing ritual of gratitude in his book about social and emotional learning. She thinks it's quite moving and decides to create a similar ritual to invite students to share stories about the ways in which their peers have been kind, helpful, or thoughtful.

She also thinks about the curriculum and instructional methods she'll be using. How might she take the learning standards for 8th grade ELA and create learning targets that invite students to explore, to create, to make meaning, and to connect their learning to their own lives and to their aspirations and dreams for the future? How might she assume a culturally humble stance to co-create culturally responsive learning targets with her students? She decides to create place-based learning experiences into which she will integrate literature and writing aligned to the 8th grade ELA standards to solve student-identified problems focused on the local community.

Londyn wants each of her students to experience joy-filled learning, and she takes this tenet very seriously. Active, relevant, collaborative, inquiry-based learning experiences are her goal. These sorts of learning activities grant students some autonomy and the opportunity to experience joy in their learning. They require seamlessly blending academic content with learning social and emotional skills.

Additionally, Londyn gives some thought to how she might co-create a sense of community through instruction. The idea that all students need to learn certain content by a certain time together just doesn't make sense to her. Students have a diverse array of experiences, background knowledge, skill, and interests that will shape how she interacts with each of them on their learning journey, the feedback she gives them, and the conversations they have with her and with their peers. Regardless of their starting point, the important thing is to chunk students' learning in ways that allow them to experience a sense of accomplishment and success. She knows this will help them develop self-efficacy.

It's Your Turn! Plotting the Course

- What do you know about the bodies of knowledge—the vertical and horizontal threads in the fabric of our sails—that inform the provision of Powerful Student Care?

- In which bodies of knowledge would you like to deepen your understanding or further develop your expertise?

- What other expertise might you add to the vertical strands of your PSC sails?

- How will you use the bodies of knowledge and the navigational instruments to ensure your students experience the tenets of community?

- How will you use the bodies of knowledge and the navigational instruments to remove barriers to the tenets of community for your students?

Gauging the Voyage Through the Student Lens

As the school year gets underway, Londyn prepares to assess how, if at all, each of her students is experiencing the five tenets of community. One fundamental difference between Powerful Student Care and other frameworks for building community she has seen is that the criteria for success are based on what the student experiences rather than the actions taken by adults. This is one of the characteristics that first drew her to Powerful Student Care. Too many times, she thinks, we gauge our success based on the effort we expend as educators: "We worked hard to establish relationships." "We don't allow harsh words and unkind treatment of one another." "I've built a safe environment." But measuring our adult effort isn't enough, and Powerful Student Care compels us to move away from the way things have always been done.

Londyn needs to understand what the classroom looks and feels like from her students' perspective. She needs to hear from students directly and often. It isn't enough for her to assume she knows how they will respond to her classroom. She needs to figure out how to actively listen. She also needs to observe, to understand students' experiences, and to plot next steps collaboratively with them.

Londyn thinks she has always done a great job of creating a safe environment for students, but she has never before thought of asking each student if they *feel* safe. Powerful Student Care has taught her to engage in the Contemplative Practice and develop the habit of mind of focusing on students' experiences relative to the five tenets. She plans to use the following tools to assist her in her PSC journey:

1. The Student Perspective Survey (Appendix D, p. 167)—she can use this survey as often as she feels is necessary to get the whole class's perspective on one or more of the tenets and the specific elements of each tenet. She can use any one or more of the survey questions as the basis for a whole-class conversation (class meeting), small-group discussion, or even one-to-one dialogue.

2. The Student Conversation Tool (Appendix E, p. 169)—she can use this resource to have the kinds of in-depth conversations she's never had with students before.

3. The Student Observation Tool (Appendix F, p. 171)—she can use this tool to watch students in action. Closely attending to how students interact with learning tasks, with one another, and with her will give Londyn additional perspective on students' experiences. For example, she can imagine gaining some insight into students' self-confidence as they grapple with a rigorous task; if students shy away from the task, she can make note of it and follow up to determine the reason and then respond accordingly.

4. The Student Product Tool (Appendix G, p. 173)—Londyn can use this tool for writing prompts, drawings, or even audio or video recordings. Its purpose is to help teachers examine student products to understand students' thinking and their experiences of the tenets of community. For example, Londyn might ask, "How did today's lesson give you an opportunity to work from your strengths and/or better understand how to work with elements that are difficult for you? How can I better support you when you struggle?" or "Draw a picture that illustrates how you understand the idea of being heard."

Students' perspectives can change quickly, so Londyn needs to be ready to see, hear, and understand each of their experiences as the year progresses. She will have to continue building, sustaining, and repairing her relationships with each student as necessary while also growing their ability to do the same with her and with their classmates. This means she needs to have regular one-on-one conversations with each of her students, and not just about school and classwork.

It's Your Turn! Understanding Students' Experiences

- How might you use the collection of PSC tools to assess how, if at all, your students are experiencing the tenets of community?

- How might you use the discrete items in the Student Perspective Survey to assess how, if at all, your students are experiencing tenets of community?

- What other methods or tools might you design and/or use to assess how, if at all, your students are experiencing the tenets of community?

- How, if at all, will you challenge your assumptions when they conflict with what students report?

- How will you respond when your students' assessment of their experience of community does not reflect the effort you are exerting to provide Powerful Student Care?

- How does your plan to understand student experience help you create your version of a "sacred space"?

Using the Contemplative Practice

For Londyn, the Contemplative Practice spurs a spirit of inquiry that helps her focus on what students are experiencing rather than just on what she is doing. It guides her to frequently stop, ask questions, and listen. It provides a disciplined process that helps her to accurately understand and respond to each student's experience relative to the tenets of community.

Londyn has clearly rejected the idea of doing things the way she has always done them. As the school year continues, she is very intentional about engaging in the Contemplative Practice to nurture and sustain that sacred space for each of her students. She commits to listening to them so she can see things from their perspective. And as she listens to them and as they listen to one another, relationships are strengthened over time. The time she uses to observe and to listen to her students is invaluable.

By mid-October, Londyn has used the Student Perspective Survey with each of her classes. She is pleased with much of the data, which indicates that students are experiencing the tenets of community. However, she also notices that her students with IEPs have communicated a different experience than the responses as a whole. She focuses her thinking on just those 12 kids, who appear to lack confidence in their ability to do well.

Londyn thinks the experiences these 12 students have had in the last eight years of their schooling has likely shaken their confidence. She decides to explore further using the Contemplative Practice to ask the right questions, learn from the answers, pinpoint logical next steps, and put her plans into action.

Londyn uses the general set of the Contemplative Practice questions (see Figure 4.2, p. 47) to help her generate specific questions unique to the 12 students. She also uses those questions to surface her own thinking about the students, about special education in general, and about her own actions as these students' teacher. As she more deeply explores these issues, she connects what she learns to the tenets of community (particularly developing students' self-efficacy and agency). She determines to what extent barriers exist for these students. She uses what she needs from the PSC sails (the bodies of knowledge), and she connects that expertise to the navigational instruments, plotting the best course for action.

Finally, Londyn takes action. She observes and thinks carefully about the impact of her actions on her students to determine how she might change course slightly or dramatically to get the results she seeks. She is intentional about noting her own change of perspective and what she has learned about herself and her students in utilizing Powerful Student Care. That is what makes it all come alive.

It's Your Turn! Using the Contemplative Practice

- How do you make sense of what you learn when you listen to your students?

- How will you use the Contemplative Practice to identify concerns about how your students experience the five tenets of community?

- How will you use the Contemplative Practice to pinpoint the most effective means of responding to those concerns?

- How will you use the Contemplative Practice to respond to those concerns?

- How will you use the Contemplative Practice to explore your mental models?

Once again, we weigh anchor and depart for our final destination: The Harbor. Here, the PSC Maritime Institute is pleased to bestow upon you the rank of PSC captain. Students will now more readily believe, and you can now more confidently say to them, "There is no one quite like you in our community."

8

May You Have Fair Winds and Following Seas

The fact that making schools more human could be considered a revolutionary thought just shows how far we are from any decent mooring.

—Professor Jal Mehta

The COVID-19 pandemic raised our awareness of the injustices and ineffectiveness that exist in the system, resulting in a glut of calls for reimagining schools. Powerful Student Care is our answer to those calls.

Despite the imperviousness of school systems to reform, there is reason to believe that educators are more willing to question the status quo and in a better position to reinvent schools than before the pandemic (Cuban, 2020; Mehta & Datnow, 2020; Reich & Mehta, 2021). If we are to take full advantage of this opportunity, our paramount priority must be to acknowledge our own humanity and the humanity of all others so that we can reimagine schooling as a fundamentally humane endeavor. To do this, we must consider and ultimately embrace what it truly means when we choose to teach.

Too many efforts to improve schooling have failed to attend to the most critical aspect of the enterprise—teaching itself (Ball, 2022;

Cohen et al., 2003). Teaching is not simple, nor can just "anyone" do it. It is about much more than simply explaining. "Teachers are not performers in the traditional sense of the word in that our work is not meant to be a spectacle...," writes Ball. "It is meant to serve as a catalyst that calls everyone to become more and more engaged, to become active participants in learning [hooks, 1994]. Simplistic notions of teaching "eclipse the sacred responsibilities of the work" (2022, paras. 14–15).

Teaching is a dynamic, relational endeavor. It requires us to approach students "in their particularity" (hooks, 1994, p. 7), coming to know, as well as we humanly can, each distinctive and irreplaceable child. It demands we safeguard and uphold each student's human dignity. As we have previously mentioned, and as we intentionally repeat here, the connection between teacher and student "is the soul of educative practice" (Olson, 2009, p. 166).

Our Theory of Action

A theory of action is a connected set of propositions, a logical chain of reasoning that explains how change leads to improved practices. It connects the dots, explaining in a commonsense way what features are expected to produce results that lead to a final desired outcome (Haertel, 2009). So, let's connect the dots. How does Powerful Student Care reimagine schooling?

If Powerful Student Care activates an unyielding proactive response to the needs and interests of each child and effectively guides educators in embodying (1) a way of being (bringing to bear our humanity); (2) a way of knowing (employing our expertise); and (3) a way of thinking (exercising our intellect) to recognize and nurture the infinite human potential of each child, *then* educators, in responding to this call, will create compassionate communities of difference within classrooms and schools that safeguard each child's human dignity; uphold each child's equal worth; and dismantle the limitations, inequities, and injustices in our current educational landscape.

In theorizing Powerful Student Care, we bring educators to a metaphorical helm where each must make a choice whether to inspire humanity in the classroom—and responding to the call will require courage.

Do We Have the Courage to Act?

If we respond to the call, we must be courageous enough to be honest about the system. Too much of what too many students experience in our classrooms and in our schools marginalizes them, harming their dignity, belonging, and sense of worth (Cobb & Krownapple, 2019; Eberhardt, 2020; Gorski, 2013; Greene, 2014; Holt, 1970; Jung et al., 2019; Kohl, 1994; Kohn, 2006; Mayfield, 2020; Muhammad, 2020; Olson, 2009; Quaglia Institute, 2020). Acknowledging that the system only works for some, we must be willing to remove the barriers preventing each student from experiencing the sense of community that is fundamental to affirming their humanity and upholding their dignity.

We must be courageous enough to be vulnerable and humble—to interrogate our mental models, question our assumptions, and commit to self-reflection and critique. It will require courage to seriously question our beliefs about students and families, to reconsider what we value and prioritize, to rethink our role as an educator, and to question our practices. Assuming a disposition of cultural humility and engaging in the Contemplative Practice support us in this endeavor.

We must be courageous enough to stop saying "we've always done it this way before." It will take courage to unconditionally welcome and value each student, as this means no longer expecting students to "fit in" or to "be fixed" as a condition of belonging. Believing in students' innate human desire to do well, even when they appear unmotivated and disengaged, will force us to be vigilant about surfacing our biases and deficit perspectives. Cultivating self-efficacy and agency entails having the courage to decenter ourselves, to engage student voice, and to grant some level of autonomy to our students. And to ensure that students experience joyful learning, we need the courage to potentially change our pedagogical practices.

If you are still skeptical about the practicality of relating to students in this powerful, caring manner, remember that "teaching is dense with discretionary spaces and teachers' everyday practice is filled with their own judgements, habits of action, and decisions that remain out of reach of external controls," and that "these discretionary spaces can be an enormous resource for good" (Ball, 2022, paras. 15–16). Powerful Student Care isn't just one more thing to put on a long to-do list, but a human journey. It is what we do in our everyday actions, in our everyday work, in our everyday interactions with colleagues, students, and families.

"Teaching, like any truly human activity, emerges from one's inwardness, for better or worse," writes Palmer (2017). "Viewed from this angle, teaching holds a mirror to the soul" (pp. 2–3). Providing Powerful Student Care to our students inspires humanity in schooling. It distinguishes between caring about and caring for our students. And in caring for students, we are compelled to come to terms with our power as educators—our power to do good and our power to harm—which may be the most courageous act of all.

The word *courage* stems from *cor*, which is the Latin word for *heart*. As Paulo Freire (2005) says,

> [Teaching] requires that those who commit themselves to teaching develop a certain love not only of others but also of the very process implied in teaching. It is impossible to teach without the courage to love, without the courage to try a thousand times before giving up. In short, it is impossible to teach without a forged, invented, and well-thought-out capacity to love. . . . We must dare so as never to dichotomize cognition and emotion. (pp. 5–6)

We think of the provision of Powerful Student Care as a form of Freire's "forged, invented, and well-thought-out capacity to love." In experiencing a sense of community, students come to appreciate our common humanity, recognizing that they and all others are distinctive and irreplaceable. We hope you'll come to the helm and choose this course. May you have fair winds and following seas.

Appendixes

The resources included in this Appendix, as well as additional resources, are available for download at www.ascd.org/powerful-student-care-resources.

Appendix A: The Five Tenets of Community

Each Student Is Supported Uniquely as Each Is Distinctive and Irreplaceable			
"There is no one else like you in our community."			
The Tenet	What It Means	What We Say Directly to Students	What We Want Students to Say Directly to Us
Each student is welcomed to be part of our community.	**If** we unconditionally extend welcome to each student by embracing each student's multidimensional identity as co-creators of a community of difference… **Then** each student feels appreciated, validated, respected, included, supported, and treated equitably, all of which contribute to the fulfillment of the innate human need to belong.	"We want you to feel you belong here."	"I am home. I belong. I have friends. I feel connected to the people here. I know people care for me and I care for them."
Each student is a valued member of our community.	**If** we categorically recognize the value of each student by affirming their inherent dignity (i.e., equal worth) as a human being through the creation of dignity-conscious relationships in an environment free of the negative role of stereotyping… **Then** each student feels sufficient safety and freedom to explore their developing sense of selfhood, experiences a deep and abiding sense of self-worth, and knows they have a seat at the table.	"We can't be as good as we are together without you."	"You care about what I have to say. I have a seat at the table, and I am heard. I can be who I am. I can become who I am."
Each student is here to do well.	**If** we absolutely affirm each student's innate human intention to do well and embrace each student's need to grow, make choices, and connect with others… **Then** each student develops an image of themselves as a capable learner cognizant of their strengths and assets and free from the harm of stereotypes and implicit bias.	"We know you come here every day wanting to do well."	"I am here because I want to do well, and I know you will help me do well. I am trusted. I am capable. I am supported."

(continued)

Appendix A: The Five Tenets of Community—(*continued*)

Each Student Is Supported Uniquely as Each Is Distinctive and Irreplaceable

"There is no one else like you in our community."

The Tenet	What It Means	What We Say Directly to Students	What We Want Students to Say Directly to Us
Each student is here to develop self-efficacy and agency.	**If** we unqualifiedly and capably foster each student's belief in their ability to thrive and their capability to do what is needed to flourish and we embrace each student's need to share the learning space with us…. **Then** each student will experience self-efficacy and agency as they feel confident and optimistic about their potential to succeed; gain understanding of themselves as a capable learner; and purposefully engage in the learning process as co-creator of the physical, curricular, instructional, and relational space.	"We want each of you to believe in your own ability to thrive as much as we do."	"I can do this. I am confident. I have power."
Each student is here to experience the joy of learning academically, socially, and emotionally.	**If** we unreservedly nurture each student's innate human desire to learn and embrace their need for appropriate stimulation, challenge, creativity, support, and choice…. **Then** each student will find their purpose for learning, make authentic meaning from their learning, and connect to other human beings through their learning, all of which together will be experienced as a profound feeling of academic, social, and emotional joy.	"We want you to think that what you are learning is interesting, that it challenges you in just the right way, and that it is relevant to your life."	"This is the place where I learn and grow. This is the place that stretches me. I am motivated here. I am excited here. I feel curious here. I feel wonder. I find purpose here."

Appendix B: The Joy of Learning

The Joy of Learning

The Joy of Learning Is Facilitated When…	The Educator's Role	Necessary Learning Conditions/ Culture/Climate	Sample Strategies & Approaches
Students experience success and the satisfaction of task completion—their self-efficacy is fortified, motivation is enhanced, and capacity to solve problems is increased.	Employ teaching methods that enable a sense of achievement of smaller learning goals within a broader learning process.	Educators work to minimize teaching that is "passivizing" and promote active engagement instead. Educators feel a synchronicity in the teaching/learning process—a sense of shared purpose.	• Problem-, project-, and place-based learning • Inquiry-based learning • STEM • STEAM • Senior projects • Makerspaces
Students are allowed an appropriate level of autonomy (choice, freedom, decision-making authority)—they are able to pursue their curiosity, use their creativity, and engage their imagination.	Employ structures, routines, and teaching methods that allow time for self-directed inquiry, free play, and "tinkering."	Educators work to eliminate authoritative teaching, understanding that joyful learning is linked to freedom. Educators view self-guided learning as mainstream rather than peripheral.	• Outdoor education • Culturally responsive and sustaining approaches • Indigenous education • Antibias/antiracist work • Interdisciplinary homework
Students engage in "a productive struggle" and successfully tackle challenging but manageable tasks where the goal is clear—they strengthen their self-confidence, enhance their self-respect, and deepen their courage to take risks; they are also more likely to experience the state of "flow."	Accurately match students' capabilities to level of complexity. Provide support in the form of scaffolding the task, accurate and timely feedback, modeling, one-on-one support, and providing adequate time for completion/mastery.	Educators need to attend to the students' mental map related to the task. Does the student view the task as a one-time, high-stakes performance, or as part of a longer-term opportunity to advance their knowledge and skill? Knowing the answer is important to reduce stress, anxiety, and encourage risk taking.	• Interdisciplinary projects • Case-based learning • Internships • Apprenticeships • Abundant and varied art and music classes • Student-led conferences • Student self-assessments • Student goal setting • Literary clubs

(continued)

Appendix B: The Joy of Learning—*(continued)*

The Joy of Learning

The Joy of Learning Is Facilitated When....	The Educator's Role	Necessary Learning Conditions/ Culture/Climate	Sample Strategies & Approaches
Students' learning is personalized—their innate desire (intrinsic motivation) to grow and strive for well-being is reinforced, they "own" their learning, and they may engage with learning for longer periods of time.	Build into daily practice strategies for coming to deeply know students. Start where students are and take them on their learning journey from there. Provide opportunities for students to practice self-evaluation as well as timely and accurate feedback on scaffolded portions of tasks. To the degree feasible, allow such stimulations as fidgeting, humming, whistling, and drawing.	Educators believe students come to school intending to do well. They communicate and demonstrate this belief to students. Educators know how to expertly use data to personalize learning.	• Recess for all! • Student voice and aspirations approaches • Cooperative learning • Socratic seminars • Student-led clubs and organizations • Reflective journals • Student-initiated units/ lessons
Students work with peers and interested, invested teachers—their joy of learning becomes integrated into relationships and their cognitive and social and emotional skills are enhanced.	Use teaching methods, routines, and structures that support collaborative learning. Minimize the use of teacher-centered, teacher-directed, or teacher-dominated pedagogy and instead facilitate learning aimed at fostering self-determination and prompting joy.	Educators unconditionally welcome and value each student. Educators facilitate a sense of community in their classroom that values and honors difference. Educators create a physical environment conducive to collaborative learning.	

Students are afforded a voice in their own learning and authority to make decisions—they develop agency for learning, are more engaged in the learning process, and make greater progress.	Use teaching methods, structures, procedures, practices, and routines that support students' innate desire for self-determination. Engage in partnerships with students to co-create learning experiences that build on their strengths, assets, interests, and aspirations.	Educators begin the teaching/learning process with the understanding that students are not empty vessels. They know the importance of accessing students' prior knowledge and attending to their interests and aspirations.
Learning is relevant to students—their innate desire (intrinsic motivation) to grow and strive for well-being is reinforced, their identity is affirmed, and their interests and aspirations are honored.	Connect content to students' interests, aspirations, cultural funds of knowledge, and personal identity. Employ culturally relevant and sustaining approaches to learning.	Educators interrogate their own mental models to surface and confront biases and blind spots.
Students' dignity is upheld—they are not self-conscious or limited by anxiety or doubt in their abilities to learn and they are able to concentrate and focus on a task.	Treat each student equitably. Facilitate antibias/antiracist culture in the classroom. Discontinue the use of practices that stigmatize, marginalize, or close off opportunities to any student. Talk to students using informational/noncontrolling language.	Educators hold equity as their central consideration in the development and use of structures, processes, practices, policies, routines, and rituals in their classrooms. Educators interrogate their own mental models to surface and confront biases and blind spots. Educators create a learning environment that is free from intimidation, stigmatization, and marginalization.

(continued)

Appendix B: The Joy of Learning—(continued)

The Joy of Learning			
The Joy of Learning Is Facilitated When…	**The Educator's Role**	**Necessary Learning Conditions/ Culture/Climate**	**Sample Strategies & Approaches**
Students are provided time for breaks from formalized intellectual and emotional engagement—their brains are able to recuperate and they are able to interact with peers in ways that synergistically support the joy of learning in the classroom.	Ensure students participate in recess and other forms of informal time, never using it as something that has to be earned or withdrawing it as a punishment.	Educators understand the benefits breaks from formalized learning serve and acknowledge that students experience the joy of learning in informal contexts throughout the school day.	

Sources: Cobb & Krownapple, 2019; Cronqvist, 2021; Pate, 2020; Rantala & Maatta, 2012; Udvari-Solner, 2012; Wang, n.d.; Wolk, 2008.

Appendix C: Quick View Tool

Our Theory of Action

If Powerful Student Care activates an unyielding proactive response to the needs and interests of *each* child and effectively guides educators in embodying (1) a way of being (bringing to bear our humanity); (2) a way of knowing (employing our expertise); and (3) a way of thinking (exercising our intellect) to recognize and nurture the infinite human potential of each child...

Then educators, in responding to this call, will create compassionate communities of difference within classrooms and schools that safeguard each child's human dignity; uphold each child's equal worth; and dismantle the limitations, inequities, and injustices in our current educational landscape.

Our Way of Being

The Tenets of Community

- Each student is welcomed to be a part of our community.
- Each student is a valued member of our community.
- Each student is here to do well.
- Each student is here to develop self-efficacy and agency.
- Each student is here to experience the joy of learning academically, socially, and emotionally.

Barriers to Community

- Stereotyping and stereotype threat
- Othering
- Violations to dignity
- Fixed mindset
- Seeing teaching and learning as transactional (versus relational)
- Deficit thinking
- Implicit bias

The Navigational Instruments for Creating Community

- Structures, processes, routines, and rituals
- Methods of instruction, feedback, and support
- Curriculum
- Power-sharing relationships
- Values

Our Way of Knowing:
The Horizontal Threads of Our Sails

Three leading-edge ideas represented as the horizontal threads in the fabric of our sails provide a strong theoretical base for realizing Powerful Student Care:

- An ethic of hospitality (Ruitenberg, 2015, 2018)
- Cultural humility (Foronda et al., 2016)
- Equity through dignity and belonging (Cobb & Krownapple, 2019)

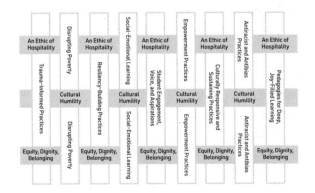

Our Way of Knowing:
The Vertical Threads of Our Sails

Woven between the horizontal threads in our fabric, the vertical threads symbolize additional bodies of knowledge that are based on research and practice from which we will also draw to support educators in realizing Powerful Student Care:

- Trauma-informed practices
- Disrupting poverty
- Resiliency-building practices
- Social-emotional learning
- Student engagement, voice, and aspirations
- Empowerment practices
- Culturally responsive and sustaining practices
- Antiracist and antibias practices
- Pedagogies for deep, joy-filled learning

Our Way of Thinking

Predict
In the Predict phase, we investigate and interpret all available information to best understand student need. Simultaneously, we surface and question our own mental models related to the student's needs and interests, together with the issues we uncover.

Plan For
In the Plan For phase, we leverage our strengths, our ways of being, and our ways of knowing to pinpoint the most effective means of meeting the needs and interests we've uncovered. At the same time, we ask ourselves why we think our intended course of action is the most effective and how these intended actions challenge or align with our currently existing mental models.

Respond
In the Respond phase, we turn our thinking into responsive action and measure its impact in meeting the targeted student need. Concurrently, we also think about our own learning and growth and whether

new learning has altered our mental models. Once we understand that our mental models can change because we've learned something we didn't know before, we realize there is always more to learn.

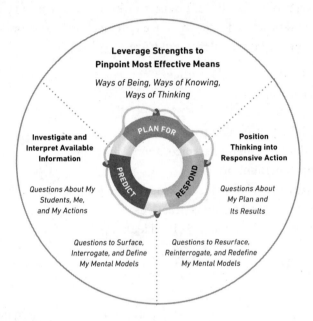

Appendix D: Student Perspective Survey

This tool can be used in its entirety or by individual tenet at any time (or multiple times) during the school year to elicit student voice. Specific items can also be used as questions during focus group interviews based on perceptions of student need.

The Tenet	Surfacing the Student Perspective
Each student is welcomed to be part of our community.	1. I feel safe at my school. 2. I belong at my school. 3. I feel appreciated and respected at my school. 4. I know people care about me at my school. 5. I have friends at school. 6. I feel connected to the people at my school. 7. I play an important part in helping people feel connected at my school. 8. I play an important part in helping people feel cared for at my school. 9. My teacher(s) know me as a person. 10. My teacher(s) care about me (i.e., my feelings, my dreams, and my problems). 11. My school is a welcoming and friendly place. 12. The adults in this school support each student by treating them kindly and respectfully. 13. Students respect and care about one another at my school. 14. I have at least one adult at school I can talk to when I need help.
Each student is a valued member of our community.	1. I feel safe and accepted for who I am at my school. 2. I am supported to be who I want to be at my school. 3. I am a valued member of my school community. 4. I feel a strong sense of self-worth at my school. 5. I am treated with kindness and respect at my school. 6. People at my school listen to what I have to say. 7. I would be missed if I were not at my school. 8. I believe that diversity in our student body (for example, race, gender, culture, disability, sexual orientation, gender identity, learning differences) is very important and should be valued. 9. I often express my belief that diversity in our student body (for example, race, gender, culture, disability, sexual orientation, gender identity, learning differences) is very important and should be valued. 10. Students in my school appreciate one another's differences (for example, race, gender, culture, disability, sexual orientation, gender identity, learning differences). 11. Adults in my school appreciate one another's differences (for example, race, gender, culture, disability, sexual orientation, gender identity, learning differences).

(continued)

The Tenet	Surfacing the Student Perspective
Each student is a valued member of our community.— (*continued*)	12. I have at least one trusted adult in the school that I know I can go to with a concern or need. 13. I believe that each student at this school has at least one trusted adult that they can go to with a concern or need.
Each student is here to do well.	1. My teacher(s) believe in me and expect me to be successful. 2. My teacher(s) support me in ways that help me reach my potential. 3. My teacher(s) know what I hope and dream for in life. 4. My teacher(s) protect me from negative stereotyping and bias. 5. My peers protect me from negative stereotyping and bias. 6. I know I can learn at school. 7. I want to feel connected to what I learn. 8. I want to feel connected to my classmates and my teacher(s). 9. My desire to do well is trusted and affirmed by my teacher(s). 10. I am a capable learner. 11. I know my strengths and weaknesses as a learner. 12. I can use my strengths to compensate for my weaknesses to learn.
Each student is here to develop self-efficacy and agency.	1. I am confident that I can do well. 2. I want to do well in school. 3. I can make the choices I need to make to do well. 4. I am able to play an active role in my learning. 5. I feel optimistic about my potential to be successful. 6. I know who I am as a learner and know what I need to learn. 7. I get to make choices about how I learn. 8. I get to make choices about what I learn. 9. I get to make choices about how I build relationships with peers and adults. 10. I get to make choices about how I sustain relationships with peers and adults. 11. I get to make choices about designing our classroom space(s). 12. I get to make choices about caring for our classroom space(s). 13. I get to make choices about how we care for one another in our classroom space(s).
Each student is here to experience the joy of learning academically, socially, and emotionally.	1. I learn in this school. 2. I feel successful in this school. 3. I am motivated to learn in this school. 4. I am challenged and my thinking is stretched in this school. 5. I want to learn in this school, even if I have to work hard. 6. I am curious to learn. 7. I feel wonder when I learn. 8. I find purpose in what I learn at school. 9. I can connect what I learn at school to my life. 10. I can connect what I learn at school to the world around me. 11. I can connect what I learn at school to my hopes and dreams. 12. My school is helping me navigate my life now. 13. My school is preparing me for my future. 14. My teachers are helping me pursue my hopes and dreams.

Appendix E: Student Conversation Tool

	Experiencing Powerful Student Care Student Conversation Tool
	Identify a student or a small group of students for this dialogue. Select a tenet and specific concepts aligned to that tenet. You can use statements from the student survey as a guide or you can create your own. Below is an example of how to use this tool with one of the tenets. A blank copy of this template for your use with any of the tenets can be found at www.ascd.org/powerful-student-care-resources.
The Tenet	**Each student is a valued member of our community.**
Conversation Topic	• I feel accepted for who I am at my school. • I am supported to become who I am at my school. • I am a valued member of my school community. • I am nurtured to feel a strong sense of self-worth here at my school.
Sample Conversation Protocol	• Greet the student and thank them for having a conversation with you. – *Hello, Willow. How are you? Having a good day? I really appreciate you taking a few minutes to have a conversation with me.* • Continue the conversation on topics that continue to build your relationship with the student. – *I saw you at the soccer game yesterday. I was really sorry we lost, but I thought it was a great game. They played really well, and I enjoyed watching it. Did you enjoy the game? Do you play soccer too? Do you like other sports too? What else do you like to do? I love taking hikes with my two dogs. They insist that we go three times a day. Do you have pets?* • Introduce the specific topic for this conversation. – *I wanted to talk with you today for just a few minutes because what you think and feel about your experience here at school, in my classroom, is really important to me. We'll have these conversations often throughout the year so that I can know as much about you and what you think and feel as you feel comfortable telling me. Is that OK?* – *Today, I would really like to talk about feeling valued. Remember how we've been talking about that tenet this year? I'd like to hear your thoughts about that. OK?* • Use a series of questions (an example follows) to start and sustain a conversation about the topic. – *We've been talking a lot about being valued. What does that mean to you?* – *Do you think that I value you? Do other students treat you in a way that makes you feel valued?* – *How would you describe who you are? Do you think that I value who you are? Do other students treat you in a way that makes you feel they honor who you are?* – *What happens that makes you feel as if you aren't valued? What would you like me to do to make sure that doesn't happen anymore?* – *What would make you feel even more valued?* – *What else would you like me to know?*

(continued)

The Tenet	Each student is a valued member of our community.
Sample Conversation Protocol— *(continued)*	• Thank the student for having the conversation with you. – *Thank you, Willow. I really enjoyed our talk. I think conversations like this are important because I get to know you better and I get to understand from listening to you what you experience here in my classroom. And that's really important to me. So, thank you very much for sharing with me today. And I hope you enjoy walking Ollie today when you get home. I'm looking forward to walking with Reva and Price when I get home too.*

Debriefing the Conversation **What did you learn about your student's experience?**	
What did the student say that tells me they experience this aspect of the tenet?	
What did the student say that tells me they do not experience this aspect of the tenet?	
How did the student's nonverbal communication provide greater clarity as to what they experience or do not experience?	
What did the student say that causes me to question what they experience?	
What questions do I still have? What do I need to explore further to better understand the student's experience?	

Appendix F: Student Observation Tool

The Tenet	What We Want Students to Say Directly to Us	What do I hear or see that tells me students experience the tenet?	What do I hear or see that tells me students are not experiencing the tenet?	What do I hear or see that causes me to question what students are experiencing?	What questions do I still have? What do I need to explore further to better understand this student's experience?
Each student is welcomed to be part of our community.	"I am home. I belong. I have friends. I feel connected to the people here. I know people care for me and I care for them."				
Each student is a valued member of our community.	"You care about what I have to say. I have a seat at the table, and I am heard. I can be who I am. I can become who I am."				
Each student is here to do well.	"I am here because I want to do well, and I know you will help me do well. I am trusted. I am capable. I am supported."				

(continued)

Appendix F: Student Observation Tool—*(continued)*

The Tenet	What We Want Students to Say Directly to Us	What do I hear or see that tells me students experience the tenet?	What do I hear or see that tells me students are not experiencing the tenet?	What do I hear or see that causes me to question what students are experiencing?	What questions do I still have? What do I need to explore further to better understand this student's experience?
Each student is here to develop self-efficacy and agency.	"I can do this. I am confident. I have power."				
Each student is here to experience the joy of learning academically, socially, and emotionally.	"This is the place where I learn and grow. This is the place that stretches me. I am motivated here. I am excited here. I am curious here. I feel wonder. I find purpose here."				

Appendix G: Student Product Tool

This tool can be used with writing prompts, drawings, or even student audio or video recordings. Its purpose is to analyze a student product to gain an understanding of how, if at all, the student is experiencing one or more of the tenets of community. Below is an example of how to use this tool with one of the tenets. A blank copy of this template for your use with any of the tenets can be found at www.ascd.org/powerful-student-care-resources.

The Tenet	Each student is here to do well.
Focus	• I am a capable learner. • I know my strengths and weaknesses as a learner. • I can use my strengths and compensate for my weaknesses to learn and grow. • My teacher(s) support me in ways that help me reach my potential.

Student Work Prompt	• Sample Writing Prompt
	  – *How did today's lesson give you an opportunity to work from your strengths and/or better understand how to work with elements that are difficult for you? How can I better support you when you struggle?*
	• Sample Drawing Prompt
	  – *Draw a picture that illustrates how you used your strengths in today's lesson.*
	  – *Draw a picture that illustrates what it felt like when you struggled during today's lesson.*

Determining Meaning What did you learn about your student's experience?	
What does this work tell me about how this student experiences this aspect of the tenet?	
What does this work tell me about how this student does not experience this aspect of the tenet?	
How does this work cause me to question what this student experiences?	
What questions do I still have? What do I need to explore further to better understand this student's experience?	

References

Achinstein, B., Ogawa, R. T., Sexton, D., & Freitas, C. (2010). Retaining teachers of color: A pressing problem and a potential strategy for "hard-to-staff" schools. *Review of Educational Research, 80*(1), 71–107. doi:10.3102/0034654309355994

Allen, K., Kern, M. L., Vella-Brodrick, D., Hattie, J., & Waters, L. (2018). What schools need to know about fostering school belonging: A meta-analysis. *Educational Psychology Review, 30*(1), 1–34. https://doi.org/10.1007/s10648-016-9389-8

Argyris, C. & Schön, D. A. (1974). *Theory in practice: Increasing professional effectiveness*. Jossey-Bass.

Aronson, J. (2004, November). The threat of stereotype. *Educational Leadership, 62*(3), 14–19.

Ball, D. L. (2022). Possible futures: Coming to terms with the power of teaching. *Phi Delta Kappan*. https://kappanonline.org/possible-futures-power-of-teaching-ball

Bandura, A. (2006). Toward a psychology of human agency. *Perspectives on Psychological Science, 1*(2), 164–180. https://doi.org/10.1111/j.1745-6916.2006.00011.x

Barron, L., & Kinney, P. (2021). *We belong: 50 strategies to create community and revolutionize classroom management*. ASCD.

Beady, C. H., Jr., & Hansell, S. (1981). Teacher race and expectations for student achievement. *Educational Research Journal, 18*(2), 191–206.

Benson, J. (2021). *Improve every lesson plan with SEL*. ASCD.

Berger, W. (2014). *A more beautiful question: The power of inquiry to spark breakthrough ideas*. Bloomsbury USA.

Brophy, J. E. (1982). How teachers influence what is taught and learned in classrooms. *Elementary School Journal, 83*(1), 1–13.

Budge, K. M., & Parrett, W. H. (2018). *Disrupting poverty: Five powerful classroom practices*. ASCD.

Buscaglia, L. (1982). *The fall of Freddie the leaf: A story of life for all ages*. SLACK.

Chandler, G. (2019, September 25). A state of mind, setting course: Teaching, learning, & leading. *Students Matter*. https://ourstudentsmatter.org/a-state-of-mind

Chandler, G., & Budge, K. M. (2020, January 20). A mission of service and equity. *Students Matter*. https://ourstudentsmatter.org/focusing-on-our-mission

Chavis, D. M., & Lee, K. (2015). What is community anyway? *Stanford Social Innovation Review*. https://doi.org/10.48558/EJJ2-JJ82

Cherry, K. (2021). What is self-determination theory? How self-determination influences motivation. *Very Well Mind*. www.verywellmind.com/what-is-self-determination-theory-2795387?print

Chuter, C. (2020, January 20). The role of agency in learning. *The Education Hub*. https://theeducationhub.org.nz/agency

Cobb, F., & Krownapple, J. (2019). *Belonging through a culture of dignity: The keys to successful equity implementation*. Mimi & Todd Press.

Cobb-Roberts, D., Dorn, S., & Shircliffe, B. J. (Eds.). (2006). *Schools as imagined communities: The creation of identity, meaning, and conflict in U.S. History*. Palgrave MacMillan.

Code, J. (2020). Agency for learning: Intention, motivation, self-efficacy and self-regulation. *Frontiers in Education, 5*(19). doi:10.3389/feduc.2020.00019

Cohen, D., Raudenbush, S., & Ball, D. L. (2003). Resources, instruction, and research. *Educational Evaluation and Policy Analysis, 25*(2), 1–24.

Collaborative for Academic, Social, and Emotional Learning (CASEL). (n.d.). The CASEL 5. https://casel.org/fundamentals-of-sel/what-is-the-casel-framework/#the-casel-5

Cronqvist, M. (2021). Joy in learning: When children feel good and realize they learn. *Educare, 3*, 54–77. doi:10.24834/educare.2021.3.3

Csikszentmihalyi, M. (1990). *Flow: The psychology of optimal experience*. Harper Perennial.

Cuban, L. (2020, August). Reforming the grammar of schooling again and again. *American Journal of Education, 126*, 665–671.

Curwin, R. (2012, March 16, 2022). Believing in students: The power to make a difference. *Edutopia*. www.edutopia.org/blog/believing-in-students-richard-curwin

Darling-Hammond, L. (1997). *The right to learn: A blueprint for creating schools that work*. Jossey-Bass.

Deci, E. L., & Ryan, R. M. (1985). *Intrinsic motivation and self-determination in human behavior*. Plenum.

Deci, E. L., & Ryan, R. M. (2017). *Self-determination theory: Basic psychological needs in motivation, development, and wellness*. Guilford.

DePorter, B., Reardon, M., & Singer-Nourie, S. (1999). *Quantum teaching: Orchestrating student success*. Allyn & Bacon.

Dewey, J. (1899/1990). *The school and society*. University of Chicago Press.

Dewey, J. (1938). *Experience and education*. Macmillan.

Dweck, C. S. (2006). *Mindset: The new psychology of success*. Random House.

Eberhardt, J. L. (2020). *Biased: Uncovering the hidden prejudice that shapes what we see, think, and do*. Penguin Books.

Fiarman, S. E. (2016). Unconscious bias: When good intentions aren't enough. *Educational Leadership, 74*(3), 10–15.

Fine, M., Weiss, L., & Powell, L. (1997). Communities of difference: A critical look at desegregated spaces created for and by youth. *Harvard Educational Review, 67*, 247–284.

Foronda, C., Baptiste, D. L., Reinholdt, M. M., & Ousman, K. (2016). Cultural humility: A concept analysis. *Journal of Transcultural Nursing, 27*(3), 210–217.

Freire, P. (1970). *Pedagogy of the oppressed.* Seabury.

Freire, P. (2005). *Teachers as cultural workers: Letters to those who dare to teach.* Westview.

Furman, G. (Ed.). (2002). *School as community: From promise to practice.* State University of New York Press.

Glasser, H. (with Block, M. L.). (2011). *Notching up: The Nurtured Heart approach: The new inner wealth initiative for educators.* Nurtured Heart.

Goldstein, D. (2014). *The teacher wars: History of America's most embattled profession.* Anchor Books.

Goldstein, S., Princiotta, D., & Naglieri, J. A. (Eds.). (2015). *Handbook of intelligence: Evolutionary theory, historical perspective, and current concepts.* Springer Science + Business Media. https://doi.org/10.1007/978-1-4939-1562-0

Good, T. L., & Nichols, S. L. (2001). Expectancy effects in the classroom: A special focus on improving reading performance of minority students in first-grade classrooms. *Educational Psychologist, 36*(2), 113–126.

Goodlad, J. (1984). *A place called school.* Perigee.

Gorski, P. S. (2013). *Reaching and teaching students in poverty: Strategies for erasing the opportunity gap.* Teachers College Press.

Greene, R. W. (2014). *Lost at school: Why our kids with challenging behaviors are falling through the cracks and how we can help them.* Scribner, Simon & Schuster.

Greene, R. W. (2016). *Lost and found: Helping behaviorally challenging students (and while you're at it, all the others, too).* Jossey-Bass.

Gregory, A., & Huang, F. (2013). It takes a village: The effects of 10th grade college-going expectations of students, parents, and teachers four years later. *American Journal of Community Psychology, 52*, 41–55.

Grove, T., & Glasser, H. (with Block, M. L.). (2007). *The inner wealth initiative: The Nurtured Heart approach for educators.* Nurtured Heart.

Haberman, M. (1995). *Star teachers of children in poverty.* Kappa Delta Pi.

Hackman, M., & Morath, E. (2018, December 28). Teachers quit jobs at highest rate on record. *Wall Street Journal.* https://www.wsj.com/articles/teachers-quit-jobs-at-highest-rate-on-record-11545993052

Haertel, E. (2009). What's wrong with inferences from test scores? Review of *Measuring Up,* by D. Koretz. *Science, 323,* 42.

Hannon, P. A., & Amidon, K. S. (2020, October 13). *Culturally competent? Perhaps. Culturally humble? Always.* www.neafoundation.org/ideas-voices/culturally-competent-perhaps-culturally-humble-always

Hattie, J. (2019). *Visible learning plus: 250+ influences on student achievement.* https://us.corwin.com/sites/default/files/250_influences_-_7.18.18.pdf

Hicks, D. (2011). *Dignity: Its essential role in resolving conflict.* Yale University Press.

Hicks, D. (2018). *Leading with dignity: How to create a culture that brings out the best in people.* Yale University Press.

Hill-Jackson, V., Hartlep, N. D., & Stafford, D. (2019). *What makes a star teacher: 7 dispositions that support student learning.* ASCD.

Holt, J. (1970). *What do I do Monday?* Dutton.

hooks, b. (1994). *Teaching to transgress: Education as the practice of freedom.* Routledge.

Iszatt-White, M., & Mackenzie-Davey, K. (2003). Feeling valued at work? A qualitative study of corporate training consultants. *Career Development International, 8,* 228–234. doi:10.1108/13620430310497395

Jensen, A. R. (1972). *Genetics and education.* Harper & Row.

Jung, L. A., Frey, N., Fisher, D., & Kroener, J. (2019). *Your students, my students, our students: Rethinking equitable and inclusive classrooms.* ASCD.

Jussim, L., & Harber, K. D. (2005). Teacher expectations and self-fulfilling prophecies: Knowns and unknowns, resolved and unresolved controversies. *Personality and Social Psychology Review, 9,* 131–155. http://dx.doi.org/10.1207/s15327957pspr0902_3

Kohl, H. R. (1991). *I won't learn from you: The role of assent in learning.* Milkweed Editions.

Kohl, H. R. (1994). Creative maladjustment. *Education Week.* www.edweek.org/education/opinion-creative-maladjustment/1994/04

Kohn, A. (2006). *Beyond discipline: From compliance to community* (10th anniversary ed.). ASCD.

Kohn, A. (2021, September 22). The case against classroom management... a quarter-century later. *Education Week.* www.alfiekohn.org/article/bd25

Kotlowitz, A. (1991). *There are no children here: The story of two boys growing up in the other America.* Anchor Books.

Margolis, P., & McCabe, H. (2006). Improving self-efficacy and motivation: What to do, what to say. *Intervention in School and Clinic, 41*(4), 218–227.

Maslow, A. H. (1954). *Motivation and personality.* Harpers.

Mayfield, V. (2020). *Cultural competence now: 56 exercises to help educators understand and challenge bias, racism, and privilege.* ASCD.

McKown, C., & Strambler, M. (2009). Developmental antecedents and social and academic consequences of stereotype-consciousness in middle childhood. *Child Development, 80,* 1643–59. 10.1111/j.1467-8624.2009.01359

McKown, C. & Weinstein, R. S. (2002). Modeling the role of child ethnicity and gender in children's differential response to teacher expectations. *Journal of Applied Social Psychology, 32*(1), 159–184.

McMillan, D. W., & Chavis, D. (1986, January). Sense of community: A definition and theory. *Journal of Community Psychology, 14.*

Mehta, J., & Datnow, A. (2020). Changing the grammar of schooling: An appraisal and a research agenda. *American Journal of Education, 126*(4). https://doi.org/10.1086/709960

Muhammad, G. (2020). *Cultivating genius: An equity framework for culturally and historically responsive literacy.* Scholastic.

National Academies of Sciences, Engineering, and Medicine. (2018). *How people learn II: Learners, contexts, and cultures.* The National Academies Press. https://doi.org/10.17226/24783

National Research Council. (2000). *How people learn: Brain, mind, experience, and school* (Expanded ed.). National Academies Press. https://doi.org/10.17226/9853

Nichols, S. L., & Good, T. (2004). *America's teenagers—myths and realities: Media images, schooling, and the social costs of careless indifference.* Routledge.

No Child Left Behind Act of 2001, P.L. 107-110, 20 U.S.C. § 6319 (2002).

Olson, K. (2009). *Wounded by school: Recapturing the joy in learning and standing up to old school culture.* Teachers College Press.

O'Neel, C. G., & Fuligni, A. (2013). A longitudinal study of school belonging and academic motivation across high school. *Child Development, 84*(2), 678–692. doi:10.1111/j.1467-8624.01862.x

Osterman, K. (2002). Schools as communities for students. In G. Furman (Ed.), *School as community: From promise to practice* (pp. 167–195). State University of New York Press.

Palmer, P. (2017). *The courage to teach: Exploring the inner landscape of a teacher's life.* Jossey-Bass.

Pate, A. (2020). *The innocent classroom: Dismantling racial bias to support students of color.* ASCD.

Postman, N., & Weingartner, C. (1971). *Teaching as a subversive activity.* Penguin Education & Pitman.

Quaglia Institute for School Voice and Aspirations. (2016). *Student voice report 2016.* https://quagliainstitute.org/dmsView/School_Voice_Report_2016

Quaglia Institute for School Voice and Aspirations. (2020). *Aspirations framework.* https://quagliainstitute.org/dmsView/Aspirations_Framework

Rantala, T., & Maatta, K. (2012). Ten theses of the joy of learning at primary schools. *Early Child Development and Care, 182*(1), 87–105. doi:10.1080/03004430.2010.545124.

Rebora, A. (2021/2022, December/January). Zaretta Hammond on equity and student engagement. *Educational Leadership, 79*(4), 14–18.

Reich, J., & Mehta, J. (2021). *Healing, community, and humanity: How students and teachers want to reinvent schools post-COVID.* https://edarxiv.org/nd52b

Rist, R. C. (1970/2000). Student social class and teacher expectations: The self-fulfilling prophecy in ghetto education. *Harvard Educational Review, 10*(4), 17–21.

Rubie-Davies, C. M. (2015). High and low expectation teachers: The importance of the teacher factor. In *Expectancies for students and others: What we know from 55 years of research.* Psychology Press.

Rubie-Davies, C., Hattie, J., & Hamilton, R. (2006). Expecting the best for students: Teacher expectations and academic outcomes. *British Journal of Educational Psychology, 76*(30), 429–444.

Ruitenberg, C. W. (2011). The empty chair: Education in an ethic of hospitality. In R. Kunzman (Ed.), *Philosophy of education 2011.* Urbana, IL: Philosophy of Education Society.

Ruitenberg, C. W. (2015). *Unlocking the world: Education in an ethic of hospitality.* Paradigm.

Ruitenberg, C. W. (2018). Hospitality and embodied encounters in educational spaces. *Studies of Philosophy and Education, 37*, 257–263. http:////doi.org/10.1007/sl11217-018-9604-9

Safir, S. (2016, March 14). 5 keys to challenging implicit bias. *Edutopia.* www.edutopia.org/blog/keys-to-challenging-implicit-bias-shane-safir

Santoro, D. (2011). *Demoralized: Why teachers leave the profession they love and how they can stay.* Harvard Education Press.

Senge, P. (1990/2006). *The fifth discipline: The art & science of the learning organization.* Crown & Penguin Random House.

Shields, C. M. (2002). Thinking about community from a student perspective. In G. Furman (Ed.), *School as community: From promise to practice.* State University of New York Press.

Shields, C. M. (2004). Creating a community of difference. *Educational Leadership, 61*(7).

Shields, C. M., & Seltzer, P. A. (1997). Complexities and paradoxes of community: Toward a more useful conceptualization of community. *Educational Administration Quarterly, 33*(4), 413–439.

Shrand, J. A. (2020, May 18). Why do we need to feel valued? *Psychology Today.* www.psychologytoday.com/us/blog/the-i-m-approach/202005/why-do-we-need-feel-valued

Slaton, C. (2020). *How school belongingness in diverse students moderates the importance of student perceptions of teachers' cultural humility in predicting student-teacher working alliance* (Publication No. 27963150). University of Central Arkansas.

Solomon, D., Battistich, V., & Hom, A. (1996). Teacher beliefs and practices in schools serving communities that differ in socioeconomic level. *Journal of Experimental Education, 64*(4), 327–347.

Souers, K., with Hall, P. (2016). *Fostering resilient learners: Strategies for creating a trauma-sensitive classroom.* ASCD.

Steele, C. (2010). *Whistling Vivaldi: And other clues to how stereotypes affect us.* W. W. Norton & Company.

Steele, C. M., & Aronson, J. (1995). Stereotype threat and the intellectual test performance of African Americans. *Journal of Personality and Social Psychology, 69*(5), 797.

Stone, P. (2011/2012). *The Romeo & Juliet code.* Arthur A. Levine Books.

St-Victor, M. & Racicot, I. (2020, October 7). Being black in media with Roxane Gay [Podcast episode]. *Seat at the Table.* https://podcasts.apple.com/ie/podcast/being-black-in-media-with-roxane-gay/id1254102196?i=1000493947981

Sufrin, J. (2019, October 6). 3 things to know: Cultural humility. *Hogg Blog.* https://hogg.utexas.edu/3-things-to-know-cultural-humility

Tervalon, M., & Murray-Garcia, J. (1998). Cultural humility versus cultural competence: A critical distinction in defining physician training outcomes in multicultural education. *Journal of Health Care for the Poor and Underserved, 9,* 117–125.

Tinkler, A. S., & Tinkler, B. (2016). Enhancing cultural humility through critical service-learning in teacher preparation. *Multicultural Perspectives, 18*(4), 192–201.

Tutu, D. (1999). *No future without forgiveness.* Image Doubleday.

Tyack, D., & Cuban, L. (1995). *Tinker toward utopia: A century of public school reform.* Harvard University Press.

Udvari-Solner, A. (2012). Joyful learning. *Encyclopedia of the Sciences of Learning,* 1665–1667.

Udvari-Solner, A., & Kluth, P. (2007). *Joyful learning: Active and collaborative learning in inclusive classrooms.* Corwin.

Valencia, R. R. (2010). *Dismantling contemporary deficit thinking: Educational thought and practice.* Routledge.

Waters, A., & Asbill, L. (2013). Reflections on cultural humility. *CYF News.* www.apa.org/pi/families/resources/newsletter/2013/08/cultural-humility

Weinstein, R. S. (2002). *Reaching higher: The power of expectations in schooling.* Harvard University Press.

Willis, J. (2007). The neuroscience of joyful education. *Educational Leadership, 64*(9).

Wolk, S. (2008). Joy: Joyful learning can flourish in school—if you give joy a chance. *Educational Leadership, 66*(1), 8–14.

Yeager, K. A., & Bauer-Wu, S. (2013). Cultural humility: Essential foundation for clinical researchers. *Applied Nursing Research, 26*(4), 251–256. https://doi.org/10.1016/j.apnr.2013.06.008

Zacarian, D., Alvarez-Ortiz, L., & Haynes, J. (2017). *Teaching to strengths: Supporting students living with trauma, violence, and chronic stress.* ASCD.

Index

The letter *f* following a page number denotes a figure.

About the Authors

Grant A. Chandler brings over 35 years of practical experience as a high school teacher, building and central office administrator, higher education dean, professional learning director in an outreach department at a large research university, technical support provider, and executive coach. He is currently the president and chief executive officer of Students Matter. He is the host of *The Wheelhouse,* a podcast currently in its fourth season, and cohost of *Abundantly Charged,* a podcast currently entering its third season. Since 2005, Chandler has provided technical support to over 300 districts in developing systemic approaches to solving student learning issues and was recognized by the U.S. Department of Education as a national expert in small learning communities. He has designed and led professional learning experiences at many levels of the K–12 arena and for many different audiences and has conducted numerous workshops at national, state, and regional conferences. His consultancies include boards of education, state and regional service providers, and individual schools and local districts throughout the United States. In his spare time, he is writing a children's book and raises standard poodles for animal-assisted activities. Contact him at grantchandler@ourstudentsmatter.org or www.linkedin.com/in/grant-a-chandler.

Kathleen M. Budge brings a blend of 26 years of practical experience as a teacher and an administrator combined with more than a decade of work dedicated to bridging the gap between the university and the teaching profession. She is an associate professor of Educational Leadership and chair of the Curriculum, Instruction, and Foundational Studies Department at Boise State University, where her research focuses on poverty, rural education, school improvement, and leadership development. Budge is coauthor (with William Parrett) of the 2012 award-winning and best-selling book *Turning High-Poverty Schools into High-Performing Schools* as well as *Disrupting Poverty: Five Powerful Classroom Practices* and the video series *Disrupting Poverty in Elementary and Secondary Classrooms.* She has conducted numerous presentations at international, national, and state conferences and served as guest speaker for webinars, podcasts, and symposiums related to the topic of poverty and the whole child. Budge's consultancies include state departments, boards of education, education associations, state and regional service providers, and schools in 15 U.S. states and 3 nations. She earned her doctorate from the University of Washington in 2005. Budge continues to maintain that her most important and significant work has been teaching 1st graders to read. Contact her at kathleenbudge@boisestate.edu or follow her on Twitter at @KathleenBudge.

Related ASCD Resources

At the time of publication, the following resources were available (ASCD stock numbers appear in parentheses).

All Learning Is Social and Emotional: Helping Students Develop Essential Skills for the Classroom and Beyond by Nancy Frey, Douglas Fisher, and Dominique Smith (#119033)

Amplify Student Voices: Equitable Practices to Build Confidence in the Classroom by AnnMarie Baines, Diana Medina, and Caitlin Healy (#122061)

Cultivating Joyful Learning Spaces for Black Girls: Insights into Interrupting School Pushout by Monique W. Morris (Monique Couvson) (#121004)

Cultural Competence Now: 56 Exercises to Help Educators Understand and Challenge Bias, Racism, and Privilege by Vernita Mayfield (#118043)

Culture, Class, and Race: Constructive Conversations That Unite and Energize Your School and Community by Brenda CampbellJones, Shannon Keeny, and Franklin CampbellJones (#118010)

Disrupting Poverty: Five Powerful Classroom Practices by Kathleen M. Budge and William H. Parrett (#116012)

From Behaving to Belonging: The Inclusive Art of Supporting Students Who Challenge Us by Julie Causton and Kate MacLeod (#121011)

Improve Every Lesson Plan with SEL by Jeffrey Benson (#121057)

The Innocent Classroom: Dismantling Racial Bias to Support Students of Color by Alexs Pate (#120025)

Keeping It Real and Relevant: Building Authentic Relationships in Your Diverse Classroom by Ignacio Lopez (#117049)

Relationship, Responsibility, and Regulation: Trauma-Invested Practices for Fostering Resilient Learners by Kristin Van Marter Souers with Pete Hall (#119027)

Restoring Students' Innate Power: Trauma-Responsive Strategies for Teaching Multilingual Newcomers by Louise El Yaafouri (#122004)

Teaching to Empower: Taking Action to Foster Student Agency, Self-Confidence, and Collaboration by Debbie Zacarian and Michael Silverstone (#120006)

Teaching to Strengths: Supporting Students Living with Trauma, Violence, and Chronic Stress by Debbie Zacarian, Lourdes Alvarez-Ortiz, and Judie Haynes (#117035)

Teaching with Empathy: How to Transform Your Practice by Understanding Your Learners by Lisa Westman (#121027)

Turning High-Poverty Schools into High-Performing Schools (2nd ed.) by William H. Parrett and Kathleen M. Budge (#120031)

Understanding Your Instructional Power: Curriculum and Language Decisions to Support Each Student by Tanji Reed Marshall (#122027)

We Belong: 50 Strategies to Create Community and Revolutionize Classroom Management by Laurie Barron and Patti Kinney (#122002)

What Makes a Star Teacher: 7 Dispositions That Support Student Learning by Valerie Hill-Jackson, Nicholas D. Hartlep, and Delia Stafford (#118001)

Your Students, My Students, Our Students: Rethinking Equitable and Inclusive Classrooms by Lee Ann Jung, Nancy Frey, Douglas Fisher, and Julie Kroener (#119019)

For up-to-date information about ASCD resources, go to **www.ascd.org.** You can search the complete archives of *Educational Leadership* at **www.ascd.org/el.**

ASCD myTeachSource®

Download resources from a professional learning platform with hundreds of research-based best practices and tools for your classroom at http://myteachsource.ascd.org/.

For more information, send an email to member@ascd.org; call 1-800-933-2723 or 703-578-9600; send a fax to 703-575-5400; or write to Information Services, ASCD, 2800 Shirlington Road, Suite 1001, Arlington, VA 22206 USA.

ascd whole child

The ASCD Whole Child approach is an effort to transition from a focus on narrowly defined academic achievement to one that promotes the long-term development and success of all children. Through this approach, ASCD supports educators, families, community members, and policymakers as they move from a vision about educating the whole child to sustainable, collaborative actions.

Powerful Student Care relates to the **safe, engaged,** and **supported** tenets. *For more about the ASCD Whole Child approach, visit* **www.ascd.org/wholechild.**

WHOLE CHILD
TENETS

1 HEALTHY
Each student enters school healthy and learns about and practices a healthy lifestyle.

2 SAFE
Each student learns in an environment that is physically and emotionally safe for students and adults.

3 ENGAGED
Each student is actively engaged in learning and is connected to the school and broader community.

4 SUPPORTED
Each student has access to personalized learning and is supported by qualified, caring adults.

5 CHALLENGED
Each student is challenged academically and prepared for success in college or further study and for employment and participation in a global environment.